It's not conventional espionage.
And it goes beyond – a long way beyond –
simple bribery.
It's the ultimate weapon in the armoury of
political corruption and subversion.
Ultimate because it exploits the most basic and
powerful appetite of humankind: sex.
It's called 'Sexpionage'.
And Sexpionage has never been so thoroughly
exposed as it is in
RED LIGHT RED

Red Light Red

As told to ALAN RADNOR

SPHERE BOOKS LIMITED
30/32 Gray's Inn Road, London WC1X 8JL

First published by Sphere Books Ltd 1980
Copyright © by Alan Radnor 1980

Printed in Great Britain by
William Collins Sons & Co. Ltd
Glasgow

Acknowledgements

For various reasons, this book has taken many years to write, and without the monumental patience and understanding of Nick Austin, Editorial Director of Sphere Books, would not now be in its completed state. My thanks and appreciation, Nick. Appreciation would be nearer the mark.

Also I would like to thank Miles Copeland, whom Kim Philby called 'that intriguer', for invaluable assistance during the early stages. Many others helped, not the least by filling the whisky glass and providing the cheering word at the right moment, including Hugh Miller in Warwick and Allen Harbinson in Cornwall.

No praise is high enough for Irene Josephy, who helped me laugh off the traumas during the writing of this book.

And finally, for the open friendliness of, and happy times spent with, the people of Montisi in the Tuscan Hills, where the book was finally written, *grazie*.

Per ognuno, tante grazie.

Contents

Foreword

In September 1973, I was Deputy Editor of a male interest magazine which obtained a world-exclusive scoop. We interviewed and photographed Norma Levy, the girl in the Lambton scandal which had rocked the British Government a few months previously. The interview, conducted by the Editor and myself, was frank and revealing.

When published, the feature gained a great deal of publicity. Letters poured into the office, either praising our scoop or accusing us of giving too much space to a woman who was 'no more than a high-class prostitute' as one writer put it.

When the last echoes of public interest in the Levy affair and our interview had apparently faded, I received, towards the end of November 1973, a hand-written letter marked 'Personal' from an address in Mayfair, London. The writer, who signed herself 'Miss B.', said that she had recently read my interview with Norma Levy, and asked to see me urgently to discuss a story along similar lines.

I sent a short note to 'Miss B.' asking her to telephone me to arrange a meeting. The reply was sent to the address given – a solicitor's office I later discovered – which forwarded my letter.

Within a week I received a telephone call from a woman who would not give her name (much to the annoyance of my secretary!) but who claimed to be the writer of the letter. She spoke in cultured English tones with a hint of a Scottish accent.

I suggested we should meet at my office but she firmly, though politely, refused to speak to me with other people around. We arranged for her to come to the office after 6 pm, when there would be no one there except myself. She agreed, so we fixed a meeting for the following evening.

The next day I caught up on some administrative work, and was still immersed in this after the rest of the office staff had left, when I was interrupted by a quiet knock on my office door. I was sitting at my desk, the door directly in front. I looked at my watch. Five past six. 'Come in,' I called. It was 'Miss B.'.

My first impression was of wealth and quiet dignified taste. She was about five feet three inches tall, and her rounded face was framed with auburn hair worn in the fashionable 'page-boy' style of the time. Her large, dark brown eyes, small nose and full mouth, the top lip a perfect cupid's bow, made her attractive, but not beautiful.

She wore a matching twin-suit – the style advertised by Harrod's in Sunday newspapers – and carried a dark blue leather handbag which matched her gloves and shoes. She appeared to be in her early thirties, and as she came across to my desk with her gloved hand outstretched, I could smell her expensive perfume – *Estée Lauder*, her favourite, as I later found out.

We shook hands, and though I tried to find out her real name, she said she was not prepared to disclose it 'yet'. She sat down in the leather guest chair, took off her gloves and kept twisting them together through her hands. She was obviously nervous, so I offered her a drink – which she readily accepted, settling for a large whisky.

As she sipped the drink, she spoke about the magazine, the Levy interview, and how interesting I must find it working in such a field of journalism, and so on. It struck me that she did not know how to begin telling me her story. She paused every few minutes, looking around nervously. 'Are you sure there is no one else here?' she finally asked. 'Positive,' I replied, but to reassure her I showed her round the empty rooms. After that she seemed more relaxed.

When we returned to my office she sat down, crossed her legs, tugged the hem of her skirt down over her knees, took a deep breath and said 'I suppose I'd better tell you my story now.' I smiled. She hesitated, probably searching for the correct words with which to begin. The office was still and quiet. The only audible sound was the hum of the rush-hour traffic outside as it rumbled past.

As she spoke I realized that if even half of what she told me was true then her story was one of the most amazing I had ever heard in my many years of journalism. She said she was an ordinary girl who had come from a normal background but had found herself involved, partly through chance and partly through design, in the worlds of prostitution and espionage. Both had been connected and she implied that she had been operative in blackmail activities at Government level. She emphasized that she saw nothing particularly wrong in this, as for years she had nurtured a personal desire to overthrow what she called the ruling classes of Britain – for reasons which became apparent later.

Some time previously she had been approached by the KGB, the Russian Secret Service*, and had agreed to become part of a secret intelligence network whose objective was to damage the British social order. This would be accomplished, she continued, by luring selected members of the so-called ruling class into compromising sexual situations, blackmailing some and exposing others.

If the plan succeeded, then the way would be open for a take-over by left-wing extremists.

Far-fetched though the scheme was, it almost came off and, in fact, its near success has been the subject of intensive study by the British Security Services and, as their guests, by the American CIA and FBI.

'Miss B.' spoke haltingly, and the small office filled with a blue haze as she almost chain-smoked through the two hours we were together on that first meeting. The traffic outside had faded to an occasional passing car. As I listened to her soft voice speaking of the terrifying ruthlessness with which the KGB had used the weaknesses inherent in any society, I found it difficult to accept the fact that she was talking of the country in whose capital, London, we were sitting, like two friends remembering old times.

* Who control the STB, the 'special arm' of Soviet Western operations.

She admitted that she 'now wanted out of the whole mess' and would tell me everything she knew – for reasons I would understand once I had heard the full story. For a share of the royalties, this young woman agreed to give a series of taped interviews in which she supplied me with all the relevant material. Naturally, names of persons and places have been changed and dates altered.

Nevertheless, the story still remains the most startling exposé to date of sexual corruption in the upper levels of British society and of the extent to which it renders the whole society vulnerable to dangerous foreign influences.

The more I spoke with her – the interviews took place at her flat over three months – it became easier to understand how she could have enticed the so-called leaders of British society into her trap. She has a charming manner, and that rare quality of keen intelligence combined with sharp intuition. That, and her ability to abstract strands of information from an apparently incomprehensible whole, made her ideally suited for espionage work.

The KGB must have realized this, and it partly explains why she was chosen to be a key operative in the Soviets' most ambitious wrecking-venture in the West to date.

Her story is to the Lambton embarrassment and the Profumo affair what the hydrogen bomb is to dynamite. But there are also incidental features. The reader is introduced to the strange worlds of espionage and prostitution: for example, the 'unworld' of secret agencies in which the Russian KGB, the French SDECE, the American CIA and the British MI6 play 'dirty tricks' on one another and generally compete in the 'game of spooks'. It also shows how officers of various intelligence services, while themselves gentlemen of high moral standards in their private lives, unscrupulously manipulate denizens of the criminal underworld to the benefit of their respective governments.

The often seedy (but fascinating) intimate descriptions of a call girl's life by a woman who only saw prostitution as a means to an end is told in frank detail. How simple it was for a well-educated, balanced young girl to become a prostitute; how she gained a reputation for pleasing her clients however bizarre their requests; how blackmail is used in the 'oldest profession' – all this is disclosed accurately with facts that have been scrupulously checked by the author and others.

Because of the nature of her work, the story contains some passages of explicit sex. This, in my opinion, is unavoidable. In fact, as she states at the end of the book, one of the main reasons for approaching me, a senior editor on a men's magazine, was to be able to tell the story fully. Had she gone to any of the Sunday papers, including the populars, she believes (as I do) that the many references to sex would have been either omitted or toned down, ruining the main point of her story – which is that, at the highest level of politics and business, men are still vulnerable to corruption if it is applied skilfully.

There is another reason why I have included most of the sexual episodes. 'Miss B.' actually enjoyed talking about sex. Her sexual exploits were more to her than mere passing incidents. They were relished by her and whenever she described them to me her tone would change. All details would be given (some of which I *have* left out). In my years in the sex magazine market I had come across girls like this who, it appeared, could gain as much satisfaction from talking about sex as from the act itself.

Apart from alterations required by Governmental security considerations (which account in part for the delay in this book's publication) the story that follows is as it was told to me. Those episodes which I felt were repetitious I have left out, along with certain autobiographical events.

For security reasons the tapes are now deposited in a bank vault. 'Miss B.' or, to give her the name adopted for the purpose of the story, Sandra Brown, has retired from the sex-subversion business, living first in Switzerland and now America. Whether she has been replaced in the secret service networks is unknown. But the fact that this conspiracy almost succeeded means that the forces working against democracy are one stage nearer total success. So in more ways than one the story contained in the following pages is 'truly horrifying' as my literary agent commented on reading parts of the tape transcripts.

ALAN R. RADNOR
London and Italy, 1978

PART ONE

Circles within Circles

CHAPTER 1

At precisely 5.57 pm on Tuesday, 14th September 1971, a black, chauffeur-driven Mercedes drew up outside a block of flats in Farm Street, Mayfair. Office workers streamed along the pavement, hurrying home on that cold night. The road was heavy with slow-moving rush-hour traffic breathing noxious fumes across this once beautiful, now fashionable part of London.

Exactly at the same time a tall, distinguished-looking man turned out of Chesterfield Hill, walking in the direction of the parked limousine, about four hundred yards ahead of him. As he approached the flats, the passenger of the car emerged and hurried towards the entrance. He was small, about five-feet-two, and impeccably dressed. His eyes were fixed on the door before him.

The two men bumped into one another. It could have been an accident. It wasn't.

The taller man apologized and waved a gloved hand towards the door. The other nodded curtly, moved ahead and pushed one of six buttons on an intercom panel. He muttered something into the grille and the door was automatically opened. The tall man watched him and when the door closed, moved forward, glanced at the panel, found the button he wanted and pressed it. A typed card beside it read 'Rochelle Duvalle'.

'Hello?' a tinny voice crackled through the small loud-speaker. 'Who is it?'

'Alexander,' the man said.

'Come on up,' the voice shrilled and there was a buzz as the door unlocked.

In the small hall he stood in front of a gold-painted gate, waiting for the lift to descend.

3

Three floors above him, the smaller man walked across to a window, looked down at his car, turned and accepted a drink from a woman with long black hair before closing the curtains.

And as the man called Alexander stepped from the lift at the second floor he was met by the other man coming down the stairs. It could have been coincidence. It wasn't.

The men nodded and silently walked along the red-carpeted corridor. Identical white doors with gold knockers and numbers stretched on either side of them. They stopped at Number 25, and the tall one pressed a small, dimly-lit, bell-push. They heard a soft chime from inside the flat and waited for the door to open.

In the street, a young man who had been studying a street directory sighed, and turned back towards his Mini parked in Hays Mews, wondering if light spot surveillance was worth all the trouble when a Czech diplomat only spent his nights with his girl-friend. Even though she was beautiful, he thought, smiling at the memory of her just before the curtains had been closed. He decided to go home, thinking how boring counter-espionage work was becoming.

The young man with romantic notions of intelligence work could have had no idea, but he had just witnessed the first moves in one of the most bizarre episodes in British political history . . .

As the sounds of the chimes died away in Flat Number 25, the woman known as Rochelle Duvalle glanced at the ornate but tasteful French ormolu clock on top of an antique display cabinet. She smiled. Just after six o'clock. Alexander was always punctual. She had known him several months, and never once on their few meetings had he been late. They had been introduced by the pianist Maria Shrimsby at a party given for Lionel Bernard when he had come from America to conduct the London Philharmonic Orchestra.

It turned out that Rochelle and Alexander had many friends in common, including one of her ex-lovers, Lord Michaels. And so, when he phoned her not long after, she had no doubts about seeing him.

Rochelle Duvalle could not be called beautiful in the traditional sense. In her late twenties, she had a well-bred sophistication and self-assurance, the products of experience. And money. Her shoulder-length auburn hair, the large hazel eyes, the oval Modigliani face and the wide, full mouth gave her a deceptive look of innocence.

At times she was like a little girl lost whom men wanted to protect, hug and caress. Or she was the demure lady men felt proud to be seen with. Always neat, always fashionable. She was the woman whose smile made men fall in love with her and whose bubbling, infectious laughter could affect a roomful of people.

She was also one of London's highest-paid call-girls.

Rochelle slipped the security bolt from its latch and opened the door.

'Alexander, darling!' she smiled. 'On time as . . .' She stopped when she saw the other man behind him.

'Don't worry, my dear,' Alexander said quickly. 'This is a friend of mine who would like to talk to you.'

Rochelle shook her head.

'Now Alexander, don't be silly. You know my rules. I don't . . .'

'Miss Duvalle,' the other man interrupted. 'It is not what it appears. I assure you, I only wish to speak with you,' he said, in a strong Eastern European accent, emphasizing each word as he spoke.

'Can we come in and I'll make the introductions?' Alexander asked.

Rochelle hesitated for a few moments and then opened the door fully.

'Okay, but I don't like it,' she muttered, her Scottish accent sounding stronger.

The men walked into the small hall, where Alexander slipped his gloves and coat off. A three-legged gilt table stood against a wall, and on it a small Capo di Monte statuette beside a white telephone encased in gold filigree. In place of the number disc a photograph of Frank Sinatra had been slipped in.

'Please come through,' Rochelle said, leading them into

5

a large, high-ceilinged lounge. A deep red wall-to-wall Persian carpet offset the gold Regency-stripe wallpaper. A white leather three-piece suite was placed round a Victorian coffee table. A collection of ivories, gilt-framed oil paintings and heavy velvet curtains gave the room a feeling of dignified comfort.

'Sit down, please,' Rochelle said, standing by the door. When she saw the men sit stiffly at opposite ends of the large couch, she felt more confident. She sat opposite them in an armchair, looking at them expectantly.

No one spoke for a few moments. Triple-glazed French windows reduced the noise of the traffic outside to a quiet hum, which did not interfere with the strains of Rachmaninoff's Second Piano Concerto which flowed from hidden wall speakers.

'Now, Alexander, love,' Rochelle finally said. 'Perhaps you can introduce me to your friend.'

'God, I'm sorry! How rude!' he said in a cultured accent, jumping to his feet. 'Rochelle, this is Simon Simenovsky, who is attached to a trade mission with the Czechoslovakian Embassy. Simon, Rochelle Duvalle.'

Simenovsky had stood up also and, bowing slightly, offered his hand. Rochelle shook it and watched the men sit back on the couch.

Both men were dressed almost identically, Rochelle suddenly realized. Black, pin-stripe suits, shoes polished to a spotless shine, dark ties – even the bottom buttons of their waistcoats were undone. The only difference she could make out was that Simenovsky had a deep blue handkerchief folded neatly in his jacket breast pocket, whereas Alexander's was white.

They look like undertakers, she thought, and smiled at the thought.

Simenovsky wore a fixed smile. He clenched his hands lightly and stared at Rochelle. His face was square, and he had black, curly hair. The colour of his swarthy skin was heightened by a long, bleached scar which ran from under his left eye to the corner of his mouth. When he smiled, the scar took away all natural warmth.

6

'Would you like a drink?' Rochelle smiled.

The men shook their heads.

'Cigarette?' she offered, leaning forward and lifting the lid off a small silver box on the table. The loose, long blue silk gown she was wearing fell open.

She was not wearing a bra. She helped herself to a cigarette and, without the slightest hint of embarrassment, folded the gown back into position. She flicked her hair back, put the cigarette in her mouth and leaned forward slightly.

Both men reached simultaneously for the onyx lighter beside the cigarettes. Rochelle's eyes laughed. Simenovsky lit the cigarette for her.

She sank back in the armchair without thanking him.

'And now, Mr Simenovsky, what is so important that you had to interrupt Alexander's and my precious meeting?' she asked. Still the eyes twinkled and danced with laughter.

Simenovsky shuffled uncomfortably and coughed nervously.

'Yes. Quite. I am sorry, but it has nothing to do with Alexander,' he said. 'I persuaded him into allowing me to meet you with him. But I will come straight to the point,' he added, speaking quickly and, Rochelle thought, a little nervously.

The music had stopped and they heard the muffled sound of a car horn outside.

'I think or, rather, *we* think that you can help us,' Simenovsky went on, his face expressionless, his dark, almost black eyes piercing her.

'Oh, really? Help? And who are "we"?' Rochelle said, not trying to hide her laughter. 'Alexander and you? I've already said I don't . . .'

'Miss Duvalle, please!' There was irritation in Simenovsky's voice, but he smiled instantly. 'I'm sorry. This all must seem very strange to you,' he added, attempting to be pleasant.

Rochelle nodded.

'I represent an international group of people called the Organization. People who . . .'

'The *what*?' Rochelle laughed. 'The Organization? I don't

believe it. It sounds like the Mafia!'

Now knowing there was no threat from Simenovsky, Rochelle began to relax. She hoisted herself back on the chair and sat cross-legged, allowing the gown to slide up over her knees, revealing her white, soft thighs.

Simenovsky sat patiently until she had settled.

'As I was saying, Miss Duvalle,' he continued. 'The Organization is made up of people who are concerned with the political state of the world. Like yourself in many ways,' he added quietly.

'Like me? Me? Oh, you can see how concerned I am,' she said, waving her hand round the room. She looked at Alexander. 'Is this some kind of a joke, darling?'

Alexander did not move.

'It is no joke, Miss Duvalle,' Simenovsky went on. 'I said people like you and I meant it. Like the people you meet every week in Notting Hill. Like the people . . .' He paused when he saw Rochelle look sharply at him, a frown on her face.

'Oh yes, we know about your political sympathies, about your leanings. Such things do not go unnoticed,' he added with a thin smile.

Rochelle grinned.

'Really, darlings. I think you're being far-fetched. I mean, because I have a few friends – no, acquaintances – who have some funny ideas, there's no need to count me among them,' she said, looking from Simenovsky to Alexander.

Neither man showed any emotion.

'I want to put a proposition to you, Miss Duvalle,' Simenovsky said. ignoring her comment. 'It's very simple, the rewards for you are great, and at last you will be doing something positive.'

Rochelle stubbed her cigarette out on the table. When she sat back she allowed the gown to stay open.

'Go on,' she muttered.

'I will try to be brief,' he said, raising his left hand and running a finger along his scar. 'Britain at the moment is going through a transition period. The political parties are split; there are no leaders of worth the people can trust or turn to; minority groups are springing up and appealing to the emotions. It is a classical situation,' he added, his finger still at his cheek. 'The moral fibre of the nation is rotting. The Profumo scandal was only the tip of the iceberg, for example. The ethics of those in power – and I'm sure you know this only too well, Miss Duvalle – are self-centred and grasping.'

Rochelle sat gazing at him, hypnotized by his quiet, insistent voice.

'And who suffers? The people!' he added, in the same firm tone. 'I ask you, Miss Duvalle, if the leadership is corrupt what hope is there for the rest of the country?'

She did not answer for a few moments, staring intently at him.

'I agree,' she nodded. 'Of course you're right. But what has this to do with me? And don't you see *me* as part of this . . . er . . . moral deterioration?' she chuckled.

'In a sense, yes,' Simenovsky replied. 'But you are not to blame,' he said softly with a smile. 'You are a victim of the system under which you live. But now, now you can use your victimization for the good of the people.'

Rochelle burst out laughing, clasping her hands together.

'My victimization for the good of the people?' she repeated. 'Give my money to charity, do you mean?'

'Please, Miss Duvalle, do not pretend to be so naïve. What were your motives when you attempted petty blackmail on Lord Malby a few years ago? And what about Sir John Aylmer Theobold? What was the motivation there? Money? Or to show up the corruption in the Establishment?'

Rochelle had paled. Her hands grasped the arms of the chair tightly.

'How . . . how . . . do you know?'

'It doesn't matter. As I said some things do not go unnoticed,' Simenovsky said, shaking his head. 'And now that we are being straight, why did you change your name from Sandra Brown to Rochelle Duvalle? Because it was more socially acceptable? Or for some deeper reason?'

'Mr Simenovsky, you're beginning to sound as if you're interrogating me. What are you accusing me of?' she asked, her eyes large, almost pleading.

Simenovsky chuckled.

'Yes, it must seem like that,' he said. 'Suffice to say, given your past, the Organization feels you can now help us.'

'How? And exactly who would I be helping?'

'The people of your country. The oppressed people.'

She stared at him as if he was crazy.

'And yourself,' he added quietly.

'Myself?' she snapped. 'At what price?'

Simenovsky looked down, and rubbed the palms of his hands over his knees.

'The price is small,' he said, his head bowed. 'Apart from the material benefits the Organization will give you – a new flat, a maid, expense account, holidays and so on – you will be able to achieve a life-long ambition.' He raised his head and stared at her piercingly. 'The ambition of easing the constant frustration you feel at the very core of yourself – the basic inability to change a system you see as corrupt.'

He paused. The quiet tick of the clock broke the heavy silence. Sandra, as Simenovsky had correctly called her, pulled her legs back and rested her chin on her knees, clasping her hands in front of her. She was shattered by what Simenovsky had disclosed about her past. And excited at the same time.

'What do you actually want from me?' she said almost inaudibly.

'We will tell you later,' Simenovsky answered. 'Let us say we want you to work with us.'

'With what aim?'

Simenovsky stared into her eyes.

'To expose corruption in most of this country's leadership. To shatter the confidence of a nation in its propped-up ruling classes,' he said quietly.

'And then?' Sandra prompted.

Simenovsky's body relaxed and he leaned back on the couch, his hands resting on his thighs.

'And then the changes this country needs will automatically

follow,' he said, a smile playing around his lips. 'When all its leaders have been toppled from power.'

The traffic was lighter as the Mercedes purred smoothly round Hyde Park Corner and headed towards Kensington Road. Simenovsky sat in the back smoking a black Sobranie cigarette and reading *The Financial Times*. A businessman returning from a normal day's work, to all appearances.

The car turned left into Kensington Palace Gardens. It stopped in front of the Czech Embassy, a grey building marked by a forest of radio antennae sprouting from its roof.

Simenovsky went to a small office on the first floor, wrote something on a pad, and dialled an internal number on a black phone, one of four phones on the desk. A few minutes later there was a knock on the door and a man in his late forties entered.

'Have this sent immediately. To the Centre,' Simenovsky said, handing over the paper.

The man nodded and went straight to the basement, one wall of which was covered with electronic receiving and transmitting equipment. The man tapped out the message on to a magnetic tape, which he then fed into a console.

The message would travel across Europe to a converted sixth-century monastery on the River Moldau, Prague. The monastery, famed previously for its magnificent stained-glass windows, now had a new reputation. Since 1961, it had been the headquarters of the Statni Tajna Bezpecnost, or STB, the Czech Secret Intelligence Service.

There, the message would be read by senior STB officers and their 'uncles', the KGB, the Russian Secret Service, who would pass it on to Number Two, Dzerzhinsky Square, Moscow, the headquarters of the KGB. Top officials of the First Chief Directorate, responsible for overseas espionage operations, would eventually read:

Cultural exchange meetings going well.
Initial interest in orchestra visit.

Translated, this meant that what was to become known as Operation Red Circle had begun . . .

*

While Simenovsky was composing his message about his meeting with Sandra, she was entertaining Alexander in the bedroom of her flat.

'Well, it was one of the main reasons I came round here,' he had said with a sheepish grin after Simenovsky had left.

Sandra hugged him.

'Of course, darling. Business as usual,' she laughed. 'My goodness! I think we could both do with a drink first after that dose of politics!'

Alexander agreed and Sandra poured two large whiskies. She did not mind in the least Alexander staying on. He was one of her straight clients, who only wanted sexual intercourse without any extras. Well, he was almost straight, she thought. His insistence that I kneel down while he enters me from the rear is hardly kinky, she told herself.

Which was why, as the message from the Czech Embassy was being received in the monastery thousands of miles away, Sandra found herself kneeling on her bed with a panting grunting Alexander behind her, both his hands spread on her buttocks, moving back and forward as if his life depended on it.

Sandra was leaning on her elbows while the good gentleman raced to his personal summit. She was thinking about what Simenovsky had said and whether he was connected with yet another cranky group she had been involved with over the years. She wondered how he had found out about her past. She was certainly not thinking about the efforts of Alexander, whose beads of sweat were dropping faster on to her back. She was a professional. And could easily attain that level of detachment which hippies and mystics practise for years to reach.

She twisted her head slightly to one side and looked at her bedside clock. Lord Johnson was due in an hour. She wondered what she should wear for him. He would want a whipping, that was certain. So she had better wear something light, as he always insisted on her beating him as soon as they returned from their night out.

She thought of Simenovsky again. What were his particular foibles? With that scar, Sandra reckoned, he was probably

12

a sadist. And then his proposition came back to her. Was he really serious?

'Sandra? Sandra?' Alexander interrupted her thoughts. 'I've finished. You've been like that for about three minutes. Is there something wrong?' he asked in an injured tone.

Sandra rolled on her back, half-closed her eyes, stretched her body and smiling softly said in a husky voice, 'Emotion, darling. That was wonderful.'

A professional.

CHAPTER 2

The following, and other first person accounts, are abridged and edited versions of tape recorded interviews made at Sandra Brown's flat in the Vale, off King's Road, Chelsea, London between November 1974 and March 1975. I have edited the transcripts to include only that which I feel is important to her overall story in relation to later events. The responsibility for this is entirely my own, as is my interpretation of the dialogue. Sandra has seen and approved the final version, however. The original tapes are now deposited in a bank vault in London.

ARR

I visited Glasgow for the first time in years recently. I went up on impulse, a whim. To see where I was born and what the old place looked like now. But it's all changed. There's nothing left of the old Gorbals I had known and lived in. Which is not a bad thing, I suppose. The Gorbals were not known as Europe's worst slums for nothing. And where our house used to stand part of a motorway now runs.

It was strange standing on the hard shoulder of the new road and thinking that so many years ago, under where I stood, Alec McNeely took me into the dunny at the age of ten and put his hand up my skirt, introducing me to a world I suppose I've never left. But more of that later.

The Gorbals I was born into was made up of long, grey tenements, common back greens and no gardens at the front. It was a madhouse of poverty, and if anyone tells you there's a warmth, an honesty, a feeling of belonging when you live in a slum, forget it. Everyone was too busy trying to survive or forget about living, to feel much concern for each other.

Look at it this way. The place was full of drunks, layabouts, petty crooks and prostitutes. The few 'respectable' people

14

who did live there liked to pretend the others didn't exist. These were the people with regular jobs whose only ambition was to get out of the place as fast as they could. Like my family, for example.

We were typically working class. My father was a cabinet maker in a local factory, and not really getting anywhere. My mother was Spanish. They had met each other during the war. She was washing bed-pans in a field hospital, to which my father had been taken after a piece of shrapnel embedded itself in his leg. From what I could gather, it was love at first sight, although I never saw any signs of this later.

These sort of things were difficult for me to find out. You see, my mother believed that sex was something a girl was told about the night before she married. That's why, she kept telling me, spinsters never had babies. When I was eight an unmarried girl in our close fell pregnant. I asked my mother how this had happened.

'The Devil, dear,' she said, puckering her dark face up. 'The Devil got to her in the night.'

For two years following I almost suffocated every night as I slept under the blankets, frightened that the Devil would come and give me a baby. And even after I saw sex for the first time when I was ten, my mother stuck to the same story.

I was on my way back from a friend's house. It was winter, the night dark and I had run home. Out of breath, I stood outside our close watching the lights and the drunks in the pub opposite our tenement. I walked into the close, feebly lit by gas, and was about to go up the first flight of stairs when I thought I heard whispering from the back green. I crept along the corridor, past the dunny, and peered out.

Leaning up against the midgies, I saw a man and a woman. The woman had her back to the brick wall. I was only a wee, thin thing at the time, if you can imagine that, and I pressed hard into the cold wall of the close.

'C'moan,' the woman whispered loudly. 'Get a move oan. It's bloody freezin' oot here.'

'Just a fuckin' minute,' the man slurred drunkenly. 'You don't want a kid, do you?'

He took something from his pocket and I heard a tearing sound. He turned slightly as he pulled something out of a packet. I gasped, and tried not to scream. Sticking out of his trousers was an erect penis! The first one I had ever seen! I was terrified. I'd seen my father's, of course – we used to share a bath at the public baths – but his was small, shrivelled and nothing like the monster about fifteen feet away from me.

The man rolled what looked like a balloon over his penis and turned back to the woman. I'd been so hypnotized by him I had forgotten about her!

She had hoisted her skirt over her waist and I made out her stockings and suspenders, could seek the dark triangle of hair between her legs. She spread her hands wide against the wall and opened her legs slightly. The man fell on top of her and all I heard were his pantings and grunts. I remember wondering how the woman was able to breathe, when suddenly he stopped, rested against her for a few seconds, then pulled himself away.

The woman smoothed her skirt while he pulled the balloon off his penis and did his flies up. She looked exactly the same as before they had started. Bored. The man rustled about in his pocket.

'There's a quid,' he said. 'I'm going back to the pub.'

I ran upstairs and over supper decided to tell my mother. Her face was completely expressionless as I described what I had seen. She didn't say anything for a few minutes.

'The Devil,' she finally commented. 'You've seen the Devil at work. Be warned.'

And then she took the family Bible down and read some passages to me, none of which made any sense.

That night I lay awake for hours under my blankets thinking about what the couple had been doing. I kept touching myself between my legs but it all seemed a waste of time. Nothing happened. No wonder the woman looked bored, I thought.

My father won some money on the football pools not long after and we moved out of the Gorbals. But not before Alec McNeely continued my rudimentary sex education.

There were about ten of us kids around the same age who mucked around together. Four girls and six boys, I think. Alec was one year older than me, and big for twelve. Well, after the usual cops and robbers, cowboys and Indians stuff, we started to play things like 'Postman's Knock' as we became older. Each boy would choose a girl and disappear into the depths of the dunny until someone shouted 'Postman's Knock' when the couple had to stop whatever they were meant to be doing.

I had no idea what I was supposed to do when Alec McNeely grabbed my hand one afternoon and led me into the damp, dark dunny. An old blanket lay on the ground. Alec squatted down on it, pulling me after him. We sat cross-legged in front of each other. I was waiting for something to happen. To feel some sort of magic sensation. Alec took my hand and yanked me across, kissing me hard on the cheek.

'What are you doing?' I asked.

'Kissing you.'

'I know that, silly. But why?'

'That's what you're meant to do.'

'Who says?' I asked beginning to feel bored with the whole thing.

'It's the rules.'

'Oh.' I couldn't think of anything to say. So I let him kiss me.

The next time we played the game, Alec said he was tired of kissing.

'It's cissy,' he told me.

'I've seen lots of men kiss,' I said.

'So they're all cissy,' was his shrewd observation, before he lunged at me and pushed his hand up my skirt, twisting his hand round between my legs. I let him do this for a few minutes, during which time he was rubbing the front of his trousers.

'What are you looking for, Alec?' I finally asked.

He stopped fumbling and looked at me with disgust.

'Is there something wrong with you? Don't you feel anything?'

17

'Yes. Your dirty hands.' And they *were* dirty, I remember. His fingernails hadn't been cleaned for weeks.

He never did tell me what he was looking for because he jumped up and walked out. We never played 'Postman's Knock' again because not long after we moved. I hope he found it, and that I didn't ruin his sex life forever.

Now it may seem that we kids had some sort of bizarre preoccupation with sex. I don't think so. We lived in the slums, don't forget. Many of my friends shared a bed with two, sometimes three brothers or sisters. Many of them also slept in the same room as their parents. They knew everything that was going on, sometimes saw it before they were ten.

Don't get me wrong. I'm not making excuses for what happened later. As I said at the beginning I'm only telling you what happened. It's up to others to work out the motives and root causes. I had enough of that in the Birdcage* when that bastard . . . . tried to make me tell him my 'motivating rationale' as he put it. But we were *aware* of sex from a very early age. I don't know if that's good or bad. As I say, we all accepted it, and copied our parents. Or rather, the others copied, and I followed. As far as I could make out, my mother stopped having sex after I was born.

Our move to a 'respectable area' put a stop to such games. The children I got to know didn't even think about sex until they were older, so I was in a pretty good position to use my sexual knowledge with Uncle George later. But I'm running ahead.

At first I wasn't too happy living in the suburbs. I missed the familiarity of my friends, found myself isolated at school – well, I felt isolated – and could not become integrated into what I now see as a sterile way of living. Sterile suburbia, I was later to call it.

About a month after moving I had my first period. I was in the toilet when suddenly this blood suddenly started flowing out from between my legs. I screamed, my first thought being that God was punishing me for letting the

* The Birdcage is a CIA 'safe-house' in Wimpole Street used for interrogation. The name of the operative is deliberately omitted.

Devil, in the shape of Alec McNeely, poke his filthy paws around my private parts.

I rushed down to my mother who didn't flinch when I told her. She gave me a tampon and told me what to do with it.

'Put it in?' I cried. 'I can't do that. And what's happening anyway?' I pleaded.

'You are becoming a woman,' she said simply. 'And when you marry you will understand fully why you have to go through this misery once a month.'

End of sex lesson!

I refused to go to school, having visions of the bloody tampon slipping out during a lesson. My father, who normally left such embarrassing topics to my mother, finally spoke out.

'It's natural. Happens to every girl. Ask and you'll find out,' he told me.

'Yes, but why? What's it all about?' I asked him.

'It's very difficult to explain. Ask your mother,' he said.

Marvellous! What I couldn't figure out was that if it happened to everyone, then why was there so much secrecy about it? I was beginning to realize that my education in some of the basic facts of life was going to come from outside the parental nest.

My father was now spending most of his time in a small tobacconist's shop he had bought in the centre of town. When he wasn't there, he would spend his time at home doing the paperwork. He certainly didn't devote much attention to his only child, and when he did, it was mostly in the shop. When I look back, I realize I never really knew my father at all.

And then they sent me away. They said it would be good for me to go to a boarding school, have the opportunities they themselves never had. But I was only twelve and already feeling insecure because of our move. I began to think my parents hated me, wanted me out of the way for some obscure reasons of their own. I created merry hell! I wouldn't eat, dressed sloppily, wouldn't help about the house or go out.

It was useless. I couldn't win. I was driven to a private girls' boarding school about fifty miles from Glasgow. And then a strange thing happened – I discovered I liked it! I had time to do what I wanted, within limits. Hopeless and uninterested in sports, I took a keen interest in English, especially literature. I read a lot, not the stuff we were doled out – Good Heavens, that was boring! Walter Scott and Dickens and people like that who had been dead for God knows how long long. No, I became excited about D. H. Lawrence, J. D. Salinger, Aldous Huxley and Albert Camus.

By the time I was sixteen, I could speak French and understood the basic principles of Greek philosophy *à la* Plato and Aristotle. The future was settled. I was going to be a school teacher, preferably in the type of school I was in. Ah, it was all so simple in those days!

Sex, of course, was almost nonexistent. During holidays I was asked out by various boys in Glasgow. We would go to parties, drink Coca Cola, listen to Helen Shapiro and Lonnie Donegan and then turn the lights out. This was the signal for intensive sex. Yes, intensive sex which meant that the boys started to frantically rub the breasts of the girls they were with, while giving them a closed-mouth kiss on the lips. It did nothing for me except give me a rash where the boys would rub my padded bra against my soft skin.

So I stopped wearing a bra to these parties. This made the boys worse. When I pointed out that I was naked under my jumper because I was fed up putting cream on my breasts the next morning, the boys laughed. And rubbed me even harder.

And then there were the car rides. A couple of boys had their own cars and we would drive down to the coast, have Coca Cola and a bag of chips and then drive back, stopping in a quiet lay-by on the way. There was one boy, Robert Saunders, who went gaga over me. He would park, get out of the car, open the door for me and then we would sit in the back. And then? Guess what? Yes, he would rub my breasts while rubbing himself against the simulated leather seat.

And once more I would wonder what it was all about.

Where was the sweeping emotion that D. H. Lawrence wrote about? What happened to the meaningful relationships Salinger described? I had no idea, but knew without doubt they were not to be found in the back of a 1955 Hillman Minx convertible, even with its two-speaker radio.

There was no point in asking my mother. She only said there was plenty of time until I got married, and not to worry about *it* before then. My father merely said 'Ask your mother. Fathers don't talk to their daughters about such things.' So when I turned sixteen, I was determined to find out about sex on my own. I bought as many books as I could, went to see adult movies, and even tried discussing the subject with other girls. Who thought I was mad.

But I had to know. You see, I was in love. With D. H. Lawrence. *Lady Chatterley's Lover* brought out more feelings of desire in me than the pawing, panting, desperate boys I went out with. Of course, and I realize this now, I was just plain frustrated. I needed what one of my revolutionary friends called 'a good fuck.' But I would take my time about it, find the right man and keep studying meanwhile.

All my plans and hopes were shattered, however. My father died suddenly. I was hauled back from school and told I could not return. We had no money and had been living on credit for years.

Daddy, it seems, was a lousy businessman. He built up debt after debt, borrowing from finance houses, building societies, the bank and his brother George to keep the house and my private education going.

He worked his fingers to the bone to keep up appearances. It was overwork and worry that killed him. What a waste! Even now, years after his death, I still feel angry. For what? Appearances! For who? Me? I thought so at the time and felt guilty. But the feeling passed when I found out what had *really* killed him. His brother George's demands for his money. Daddy just couldn't pay. But George insisted, although I reckon he didn't really need the money. Especially when it turned out George wanted it for a holiday in Italy!

Daddy couldn't sleep or work properly. And when the heart attack inevitably came, he must have felt relief to be getting out of it all.

I hated the whole world. Everything seemed to go on in the same way, as if my father had never existed. Okay, I wasn't that close to him, but I had enough maturity to see he had tried his best for his family. It was so unfair. And no one seemed to be interested. I was furious. I wanted to kick out at everything, smash the indifference around me. But then, I was only sixteen.

Too young to realize death is a natural part of life; too old to be fobbed off and told Daddy was going to Heaven. It was too vague. I couldn't understand at all. Uncle George provided the way out. It was all his fault. He was the one who had killed Daddy. It was simple. Now I could understand. And pay him back for what he had done to us.

Uncle George had been married for fifteen years and had two sons, one thirteen and the other ten. He liked to crack crude, obscene jokes and would laugh at them himself. He was tall, and had deep brown eyes, a bit like my own. He must have been good-looking at one time, though when I was sixteen he was developing a slight paunch.

What amazed me, even then, was he didn't seem to do anything. He owned a clothing shop and when he wasn't in it he would loll about the house watching television or cleaning his car. Quite honestly, I thought he was a slob. I couldn't stand watching him eat the huge meals my aunt, a fat little lady who fussed more about her children than herself, would cook for him.

But he was the man who killed my father. And I was going to be his Lolita. I had read the book about three times at boarding school, excited by what Nabokov was saying about women, and what they could do with their bodies.

I had no definite idea of what I was going to do, of course. I lay awake night after night planning the most vile tortures which included masked Chinese bandits and members of the Mafia. And then it came to me. Lolita had used her body, so why shouldn't I? I would trap Uncle George by using my then fairly well-developed body! It was obvious. I worked the whole scheme out, running over it in my mind about a dozen times.

It was so beautifully simple! Even Kosca during my training much later congratulated me on the scheme.

I had just enrolled at a co-ed adult education college, so had plenty of time during my studies to refine my plot. I mixed with a few other students and sat around in the coffee shop with them arguing about the state of the world, how rotten the system was, and what was needed was a revolution which would be something positive.

I realize now they were opportunists, or revisionists as Mao Tse-Tung would have called them. On the one hand they slammed the State system but on the other they were all taking grants and living off the Establishment. But I was introduced to a whole new set of ideas and jargon which seemed to make sense to me at the time.

And of course, when they talked about 'the moneyed classes' using and destroying the working classes, I translated these general phrases into my own particular situation. Uncle George became the capitalist, one of the bourgeoisie, who milked poor workers like my father. And hadn't he almost destroyed our family because of money? And so, although I couldn't accept *everything* that Marx and Lenin put forward – to be honest, I couldn't understand it all – I felt a lot of it was right. The sooner people like Uncle George were shown up to be what they really were, the better, as far as I was concerned.

I saw Uncle George as often as I could. I would pop into his shop on some pretence or other wearing a mini-skirt, a style which was just becoming fashionable. He kept a pile of *Playboys* in the shop and once or twice I had caught him ogling them, when he would become embarrassed.

I touched him a lot, and told him now that Daddy was dead how good it was to have someone to give me advice. And whenever I left him, I gave him a little kiss on the cheek.

A couple of times I let a week or two slip by without seeing him. When I went to the shop he would say how much he had missed me. Which was why I had left him alone, of course.

I would deliberately drop things in front of me and bend down, letting him see my skimpy panties. It was obvious he was affected, because once I turned round and quickly noticed the tell-tale bulge in the front of his trousers. One of the disadvantages of being a man, I thought!

When I visited their home, I would help my aunt with dishes and clearing up and talk to her as often as I could. I listened patiently as she lectured me on the way I was dressing, and how I would get into trouble if I wasn't careful. I would nod, agree and promise to think about it. But as I kissed Uncle George good night, and saw his eyes hungrily peer down my loose blouse, I knew the 'outfits' would have to stay a little longer.

One evening, while my mother was in Spain visiting her family, I stayed on later than usual at Uncle George's place watching television.

'Could you run me home, please, Uncle George?' I asked eventually. 'It's so late and I'm tired.'

'Why don't you stay here?' my aunt suggested.

'There's an early lecture tomorrow and I've got to change,' I lied.

During the drive, I pretended to be sleepy and put my head on Uncle George's shoulder. I curled up on the seat, letting my skirt ride high up my thighs.

Uncle George muttered something about me catching cold and leaned over to the back seat and pulled a rug across. With one hand he covered me with the rug. But in doing so, he 'accidentally' brushed his hand against my thigh. I moved a little, and the rug slipped. He went to put it back, but this time his hand stayed a little longer on the soft inside of my thigh. I moaned as if I was dreaming, and closed my legs on his hand. And instead of trying to slip it out, he pushed along my thigh, almost to my knickers. It was so easy, I lay thinking!

I felt the car slow down and opened my eyes.

'Are we here already?' I yawned, 'I must have fallen asleep.'

My uncle's hand shot out from between my legs and he grabbed the rug.

'The rug,' he said nervously. 'You could catch cold.'

'Thank you,' I smiled and kissed him on the cheek before

running into my house.

The rest really was like taking sweets from a baby. And I thought men were strong! There were lots of little ploys like the one I've just described but the one I remember best and that gave me lots of laughs later was the night we drank a bottle of wine between us.

My mother, who seemed to have relatives all over the world, including Newcastle, had been invited there by yet another of her sisters. I insisted she went, telling her I had plenty of work to do for college.

She was away a few days when I decided it was time to see George again. I pulled the wires out of the fridge plug.

'Uncle George,' I said sweetly when I phoned him. 'There's something wrong with the fridge and all the food's going off. Could you come and look at it?'

He arrived within minutes and fixed the plug.

I offered him a glass of wine, and as I already had one in my hand, he agreed to have 'just one glass.'

An hour later we had finished the bottle. I was giggly but not drunk. Uncle George, who hardly drank, staggered slightly as he stood up. I put my arms around him, holding him tightly.

'You're not drunk, I hope?' I laughed.

He shook his head.

Then I slumped against him.

'Oh, Uncle George, I feel ill,' I moaned. 'Can you get me upstairs, please?'

He half-dragged, half-carried, me upstairs, one hand resting on my buttocks and the other across my back.

He laid me on my bed. I moaned loudly, trying to pull my jumper off.

'What's happening?' I acted. 'It's so hot.'

You should have seen his face! Was he worried! Goodness, I thought *he* was going to faint. He kept shrugging, not knowing what to do.

'Wanna sleep. Wanna sleep,' I kept mumbling, watching him through my practically closed eyes.

'Oh God. Oh God. Jesus Christ. Jesus Christ,' was all he would say, like a mad priest.

I never stopped tugging at my clothes, and finally he decided to help me undress. Unzipping my mini-skirt, he slid it down over my legs, and then pulled my jumper over my head. I was left in my bra and pants.

He looked down at me for a few seconds. I could just imagine what was going through his mind. I sat up and put my hands round his waist.

'Oh, Uncle George, I'm sorry. I'm so sorry. I didn't mean to get drunk. I feel terrible. You won't tell Mummy, will you? Promise.'

'There, there,' he muttered, stroking my hair as if I was about to die.

I pressed my breasts close to him and felt his stiffness against them. Moaning quietly, I moved backwards and forwards, rubbing myself against his penis. Suddenly he gasped and almost jumped away.

'I've got to go,' he said rushing out of the door. 'You go to sleep.'

Sleep! I was up the second I heard the front door slam. I rolled about the floor laughing like a lunatic. I knew he was ready to be taught his lesson at last. I was so excited, both from the thought of what I was going to do to him and the way I had been aroused by rubbing against his penis. I masturbated before I went to sleep, which seemed to help relax me.

I had to move quickly after that night. My mother was returning home at the week-end to prepare for my birthday party the following week when I would be seventeen.

I phoned George at his shop.

'How would you like to give me a birthday treat, Uncle George?'

He didn't answer.

'There's an absolutely super new play on at the Citizen's Theatre.' I went on. 'All my friends are busy and tomorrow's the only night I've got free for a while. How about taking me tomorrow?'

'Oh, I don't know . . .' he said.

'About last night, Uncle George . . .'

'Yes?' he almost screamed down the phone.

'You were so kind,' I purred. 'I'm so sorry if I caused you any trouble.'

'Yes, well. That's okay.'

'What about tomorrow night?'

'Your aunt doesn't like theatre,' he said. He was hedging. And I knew perfectly well my aunt couldn't stand going to the theatre.

'Well, you take me. Say you've got to see a buyer or something. Oh, please, Uncle George. It would be so nice.'

'Okay. I'll pick you up after the shop closes, about half past six.'

'Oh, thank you. Thank you.'

I couldn't believe it. It was all working out as I had hoped. That night I couldn't sleep, no matter what I did. The next day dragged. I checked twice with Uncle George to make sure he was coming.

I knew it took half an hour to reach our house from his shop and at about quarter past six I phoned the business. There was no reply. He was on his way.

I immediately phoned my aunt, pretending to be crying.

'Oh, I'm in such terrible trouble,' I wailed. 'I'm trying to make a dress for my birthday party and it's not working out. Could you help me, please?'

'I'll pop around at the week-end and have a look at it,' she said.

'Oh no, that's too late,' I cried. 'I want to have it ready as a surprise for Mummy when she gets back. I was going to finish it tonight.'

'Oh, all right. I'll be round in a while.'

'What time?'

'About nine.'

'Oh good. Thank you.'

When my uncle appeared at half past six, I was sitting looking miserable.

'They're all sold out,' I said. 'Not a ticket left. I'm fed up,' I said, pouting my lip. 'I was so looking forward to it.'

He shrugged.

'Oh, well. I'd better go home.'

'Have you eaten?' I asked quickly.

'No. I'll eat when I get back.'

'Well, listen,' I said, jumping up. 'Why don't we try that new Chinese place round the corner? I'm starving. And it *would* make up for the theatre.'

'What a silly little girl you are,' he grinned. 'Okay, let's go. Uncle George's treat,' he said, patting me on the bottom.

We had a bottle of wine with the meal, on my insistence.

'I'm only having two glasses, Uncle George. You remember what happened last night?' I reminded him, smiling sweetly.

He blushed. He actually blushed!

'I'm really enjoying myself,' I told him truthfully. But for different reasons than he imagined . . .

When we reached home, he was again slightly tipsy. The evening was chilly and I turned the heating full on in the front room. I glanced at the clock. Nearly half past eight.

'That was lovely, Uncle George. Before you go would you like some whisky? An advance toast for my birthday.'

'I shouldn't, you know, but what the hell!' he laughed.

After drinking nearly a bottle of wine at the meal, I knew he shouldn't drink whisky as well. Which was why I poured him a large scotch. I had a Coke.

He lay back on the couch, the wine and whisky beginning to affect him. I sat at his feet, lightly rubbing my fingers along the inside of his thigh.

'I feel so much better now,' I said, laying my head on his lap. My cheek rested against his penis, which was, as I expected, erect. I moved my head round, pressing into him.

George did not move. He had finished his whisky and lay back, his eyes closed.

'I'm so comfortable,' I said, and put one hand between my cheek and his penis and snuggled closer.

He started to move my hand away but stopped. I was rubbing my hand along him.

'Sandra, what are you doing?'

'Oh, nothing,' I said innocently. 'Is it nice?'

'That's not the point. You're my niece.' But he didn't make any move to stop me.

'I don't know what you mean, I'm sure. We're not doing

anything *wrong*, are we?' I asked.

'No, of course not. But you are a young very attractive girl and I'm a man. And, and . . . and . . .'

He stopped when he felt me unzip his fly. His hand shot down.

'No! Stop it!' he ordered me. But he still didn't move.

'I just want to see what it looks like, *Uncle* George. The girls at college talk about them, and I've never seen one,' I lied, as I pulled his pants to the side.

I must admit he was fairly well endowed. I ran my fingers up and down his penis softly. He lay back, his eyes closed, mumbling something about all this being wrong.

What he didn't see was me unbuttoning my blouse. And looking at the clock. Five to nine. I pulled my blouse out of my skirt. I was braless and my breasts hung down.

I took one of his hands and laid it on my left breast.

'Sandra!' he gasped, but he was too far gone between the drink and my rubbing to do anything about it.

I was beginning to get excited myself, when I heard the door open behind me.

'George!' my aunt screamed.

He froze, and I felt his whole body stiffen. I jumped up and ran across to my aunt.

'Oh, thank goodness you've come,' I sobbed. 'Thank goodness. I'm so frightened. He came around here just after I spoke to you and took me for a meal. He gave me lots to drink – and you know I don't drink – and then told me unless I did things to him he would have my mother and me thrown out of the house. I feel so ashamed.' I was actually crying.

My aunt wrapped her arms round me and told me everything would be all right.

George had stood up by this time, and was zipping up his flies, looking completely confused.

'Get out! I never want to see you again, you filthy creature!' my aunt yelled. 'Don't ever come near me or my children as long as you live, you despicable filthy bastard!'

Uncle George shambled past us without saying anything. He was shaking his head, not quite believing what was happening.

They were divorced soon after. I, of course, let everyone know what he had tried to do to me. They all felt sorry for me and would not believe *his* version. When the word spread round no one wanted to deal with Uncle George and he had to close his shop, most of the money going to my aunt. Eventually, he left Glasgow and I haven't heard of, or from, him since. And I don't particularly want to.

Of course, as Kosca pointed out to me when I told him the story, I blew it. I shouldn't have phoned my aunt. That way, I could have blackmailed Uncle George. But my mind didn't work along these lines in those days. I had decided to leave for London, and it was there, with much bigger fish than Uncle George, I was to find out exactly what Kosca was talking about.

Although I almost did stay in Glasgow. After my little performances with Uncle George and my aunt, I seriously considered enrolling at the Royal College of Music and Drama, seeing myself as an actress.

But I suppose when you think about it, I'm not so far removed from that profession after all . . .

CHAPTER 3

Simon Simenovsky sucked noisily on a large Havana cigar and stared at the man opposite him. They were sitting at a low coffee table in a corner of the Czech's office. On the table was a bottle of vodka, two glasses and a thick, buff-coloured dossier.

The office was not sumptuous, but compared to normal STB and KGB standards it was luxurious. A few Persian rugs were scattered over the deep green wall-to-wall Axminster carpet; a large mahogany bow desk stood in front of the window, a leather executive chair behind it; a battery of coloured phones were lined up on the desk; the oak-panelled walls were hung with gilt-framed oil paintings of Czechoslovakian and Russian scenes, alongside two large prints of Lenin and Leonid Brezhnev.

'Well? What do you think, Viktor?' Simenovsky asked the other man, speaking from the corner of his mouth while biting on the cigar.

'I think you're right, Simon. She's certainly recruitable. And she seems willing enough to co-operate,' Viktor said. 'There's only one thing that troubles me . . .'

'What's that?' Simenovsky asked quickly, grabbing the cigar from his mouth.

Viktor noticed the nervousness but did not comment on it.

'It seems too good to be true,' he said. 'I know, I know. You're going to quote School 101's Recruitment Programme at me about an ideal agent being one who has sympathies towards the USSR as a consistent striver for peace,' Viktor smiled. 'But is that enough? A single motivational factor? I can't see it,' he added, shaking his head.

Simenovsky drummed his fingers impatiently on the arm

of his easy chair.

'Oh, come, come, Viktor, do you think we're that naïve?' he laughed. A dry, brittle laugh. 'Of course she's not the dedicated political animal she likes to think she is. Sandra Brown is as interested in money as every other capitalist. Her working-class background only produced in her a desire to denounce it. Her flirtations with the leftist movements are only token gestures. No, we will offer to pay for her flat, completely refurnish it from an account to be opened at Heals or Harrods, we're going to pay for a full-time maid – provided by us, of course. Sandra can open an account for clothes, travel, gifts and restaurants up to £500 a month. And naturally, all bribes which may be necessary will be met by us. That's our real bait.'

Viktor nodded.

'It sounds good. Makes me wish I was an agent instead of a training officer,' he laughed.

When he saw Simenovsky did not respond, he quickly added he was only joking.

'I should think so, Viktor. With your style of life, I think you have no complaints.'

'Now what?' Viktor asked, changing the subject.

'It's time for you to have your first meeting with her,' Simenovsky said. 'I've chosen a safe-house in Bayswater. You . . .'

'Bayswater? You must be joking. I wouldn't be seen dead in somewhere like Bayswater. And neither would someone like Sandra.'

'Exactly. That's what I thought. So there is no chance you'll run into someone you know. Right?'

'I suppose so,' Viktor grumbled. 'Bayswater!'

'I'll see her this evening . . .'

'Professionally, I trust,' Viktor smiled.

'Very amusing. Even your jokes are becoming Western-ized,' Simenovsky retorted. 'Perhaps you've been here too long,' he added in an icy tone. 'As I was saying, I'll arrange the meeting for tomorrow morning, if that fits in with your plans.'

'Fine, fine. Does she know who she's working for yet?'

Simenovsky shook his head.

'She still thinks she's helping the Organization. You can tell her the truth tomorrow.'

Viktor nodded.

'You do realize, Viktor, how big this could be?'

There was no humour in Viktor's voice as he answered.

'I'm not a child, Simon. I know only too well. It could be the beginning of a fine Party career for us all. Or the end.'

Sandra had not heard from Alexander or Simenovsky for ten days after their visit. She was beginning to think the whole thing some sort of elaborate joke, when Simenovsky appeared on her doorstep.

'I'd given you up, darling,' she smiled when they were seated in the front room.

'I wanted to give you time to think about helping us,' he said flatly. 'Have you decided?'

'It all sounded marvellous, but then so have a lot of other movements I've been involved with. Which got me nowhere as far as a *revolution* is concerned,' she laughed. 'And I always seem to end up in bed,' she bubbled.

'Quite. As I said at our last meeting, you are a victim of the system. You . . .'

'Don't get me wrong, love,' she laughed, clapping her hands together. 'I don't mind. As long as I've got freedom to choose who I'm going to bed with!'

Simenovsky was silent. He had been brought up in Czechoslovakia and Russia, and although he had spent three years in London, he still found Western sexual promiscuity, as he saw it, hard to accept. It irritated him for two reasons. Firstly, as a good Party member he viewed sexual permissiveness as another sign of Western capitalist degeneration. And secondly, he wanted a slice of it himself but could not have it because of his position as an STB case officer in London.

'You are seeing Lord Phillips tonight, I believe,' he said.

'Good Heavens above! How did you know that? Don't answer. Some things don't go unnoticed as you said last time,' she smiled. 'And don't look so surprised, darling. I've got a good memory for some things.'

Simenovsky, a man not given to much humour, chuckled.

'Yes, we know. Now, I have a simple request,' his face straight again. 'I would like you to find out where Lord Phillips will be having lunch tomorrow. One of the Organization may wish to approach him. Accidentally, of course.'

Sandra looked at him in surprise.

'Is that all? That's no trouble, my love. Will I phone you?'

'No, no. I'll call you in the morning.'

That night, as Lord Phillips and Sandra sat at a quiet corner table in Tramp, a smart night-club in central London, she was not thinking of Simenovsky's request. She was concentrating on pleasing his Lordship. She met Phillips about once every two weeks. In his forties, he was married to a society lady whom he rarely slept with, he admitted to Sandra. For £100 she would be taken for dinner and while the good Lord stroked her thighs under the table – always insisting she wore stockings and suspenders – Sandra would provide a fantasy for him. Nothing more. There was no sex between them. Sandra never asked why, nor what he achieved later from the fantasy. If that's what he wanted, she reckoned, then she would provide it.

The fantasy that evening involved one of Phillips's favourite images – a French maid in frilly underwear, short black skirt and black nylons and suspenders. Breathlessly, Sandra described how his Lordship had come home early to find the girl in her room, panties about her knees, and furiously masturbating herself. Phillips would then take her hand away from her vagina and place it over his penis, which led to wild abandoned love-making.

As Sandra described all this, her face alternated between pleasure and excitement. His Lordship's hand would move faster, often touching her own dampness. Sandra would never laugh, or turn the fantasies into farce. They were the props certain men needed, she knew.

The night-club or restaurant was the couch; she the sympathetic psychiatrist.

Phillips hung on to every word, grunting and nodding through the story. When she had finished, he was breathing deeply.

'Thank you, my dear,' he said quietly. 'Thank you. That was superb.'

'My pleasure, darling, I assure you,' she smiled. 'I enjoy my nights out with you. Listen, darling,' she said leaning forward. 'I'm going shopping tomorrow. Why don't we have some lunch together?'

'Oh, I'm sorry, Rochelle, I'm booked up. Another time perhaps.' His hand still rested inside her thigh, and he squeezed her gently. 'It's a nice thought.'

'You won't be near Harrods, will you?' she asked, taking a shot in the dark.

'No, love, I'm seeing some chap from British Steel at Les Ambassadeurs. Sorry.'

Her face puckered with disappointment.

'Ah, well, another time.'

On the way back to her flat in Phillips's Bentley, he handed her a sealed envelope without a word. At the flats, she kissed him lightly on the cheek and ran to her door, waving as he drove off. Inside, she put the envelope in a drawer of a Louis XV table. She did not open it, knowing what was inside. Ten crisp ten-pound notes. There was no need to count it. Sandra's clients never caused problems with money.

The phone rang just after nine o'clock the following morning.

'Well, did you find out?' Simenovsky barked.

'Don't be so grumpy, love,' Sandra replied. 'Of course I found out. And guess what? Not only did I find out *where* he was having lunch, but with *who*,' she said excitedly.

'Excellent, excellent,' Simenovsky commented.

Sandra gave him the details.

'Your . . . er . . . compensation for your trouble will be sent to you this afternoon.'

'Trouble? It was no trouble, believe me. If that's all I have to do to help you, then I'm more than willing.'

Simenovsky did not reply. A thin smile of satisfaction was spreading across his face.

'Good. I'll be in touch shortly,' he said and hung up.

Later that day Sandra found a white envelope in her

mailbox. Inside was £50. A typed note with the money simply stated: 'Thank you. S.'

Over the next few weeks, Sandra was asked for little snippets of information similar to the one about Lord Phillips. And always, after she had provided it, an envelope with £50 would arrive. She could not believe it. It was all so easy. Soon she felt nothing about steering a conversation towards a particular angle. Any pangs she had had about giving private information to the Organization soon disappeared when she found how simple the whole process was.

Which was exactly what Simenovsky and his bosses at The Centre in Prague wanted. All the information Sandra gave them was useless. They were broadening her area of conscience, giving her time to justify to herself that what she was doing was not wrong, could do no harm. Sandra was being treated like any other prospective agent. Which she, as yet, could have no way of knowing.

Viktor Pavlenko enjoyed life. Although a self-confessed Communist, he had ingratiated himself into London's jet set. He was, and knew it, their pet Commie. He was to be seen at the rich and fashionable gatherings in Belgravia and Chelsea; playing the tables at the exclusive gambling clubs in Curzon Street; dancing in the society night-clubs and eating in the top restaurants. At cocktail parties he would tell amusing stories about Communist leaders. He was head of a Czech travel agency in London, and to all appearances, a playboy.

He was also a highly-trained intelligence officer for the STB. Everything he did was an act, a pose for the benefit of the wealthy, bored jet setters. For the gullible.

Over six feet tall, with fair hair and deep blue eyes set in a square face, he looked more English than Czech. He always had a quip or a joke at his lips. His accent would sound perfect, although sometimes he would stumble over words and phrases. A ploy to gain sympathy. He was popular at parties, not only because of his generosity at providing caviar, but also 'because he's such a natural English gentleman,' as one titled lady described him.

Which was the result of four years' intensive training in Russia.

Viktor drank only tonic water at the many functions and parties he attended. Then he would return to his Chelsea flat and write down everything he had heard and seen that night. For, as he knew only too well, expertly collected trivia often point to hard facts, or give leads to them.

Sandra had come across Viktor during her Chelsea days, and thought him a friendly, witty playboy. She had no idea he was a Czech, and it would have made no difference if she had.

So she was delighted when, on the instructions of Simenov-sky, she met Viktor in the Bayswater safe-house.

'You're in the Organization as well?' she asked in surprise.

Viktor nodded.

'Oh, how wonderful! We'll have some fun, then,' she laughed.

Viktor did not respond.

'We have a great deal of work to do, Sandra,' he said firmly. 'There won't be much time for fun, I'm afraid.'

'But, darling,' she protested, an impish smile on her face. 'What's happened to you? Where's the happy-go-lucky, carefree Viktor I used to know? Do you remember those parties Anthony used to give? When you . . .?'

'We are not at a party now, Sandra,' he said.

'Well, for goodness' sake! Do you mean it's all going to be work between us?'

They were sitting in the front room of the house, actually a small flat. A cheap three-piece suite, a table and a radio set were the only furniture in the room. Sandra was perched on the couch, wearing a woollen jumper, tweed skirt and a mink coat. She settled back in the couch, and crossed her legs, allowing Viktor to see her thighs and blue nylon panties.

He gave no indication of even noticing. Sandra was amazed at the change in him.

'I'd better begin by telling you about the Organization,' he said and explained it was in fact the STB, backed by the KGB.

Sandra was thrilled. The thought of working for a world-wide, influential, powerful organization aimed at changing political systems made her feel important. Worthwhile. She was doing something positive.

Exactly the reaction Simenovsky and Viktor Pavlenko had anticipated.

'I'll give you lots of bits and pieces, if you like,' she said, reaching for her handbag. 'I'll take your number and call you when anything interesting comes up.'

'No!' Viktor said angrily. 'That's what we don't want. It's been very easy up to now.' He paused when he saw Sandra staring at him. 'And it can be easy in the future. You'll have all you want – money, security, a sense of well-being. But only as long as you follow our orders. Stick to the rules, Sandra, and you have our backing, our protection. Break one of them, and you're on your own. Don't look to us for help. Do you understand?'

Sandra nodded silently. She was beginning to realize there was more at stake than she thought. Again, this was the purpose of Viktor's bitter-sweet talk.

'Good, we can start now,' he said relaxing. 'First of all let me say how sorry I am about having to meet here, but I can assure you it wasn't my idea.'

'Oh, I don't mind,' Sandra said. 'It's hardly my idea of heaven, but you know best.'

'Exactly. And that's why I'm furious about Simenovsky choosing this ridiculous hide-out.'

'Now, now, darling. Don't get flustered.'

Viktor scowled at her flippant remark.

'You don't understand,' he said. 'Meeting in a place like this breaks Rule Number One of espionage communications. You should always meet openly, with some acceptable business or social excuse,' he went on. 'Or in complete secrecy in some place to which the approaches can be made in the course of normal events. We both had to come out of our way to come here. Which is not only ridiculous, but damned dangerous.'

Sandra stared, wide-eyed, at his outburst. She caught the drift of what he was saying, even if she couldn't understand everything he was talking about.

She was taking her cigarette case out of her bag when Viktor suddenly put both his hands over his tie.

'Tell me what colour my tie is,' he demanded.

Sandra was taken aback. His waistcoat hid all signs of it.

'It's blue with little brown squiggly things on it,' she said, looking puzzled.

'You're off to a good start,' he smiled. 'Most people couldn't answer that question. They can't even tell you the colour of their *own* dresses or shirts without looking down to check.'

Sandra lit a cigarette, wondering what was coming next.

'Can you describe Annabelle's Club to me now?'

She did so and Viktor sat nodding as she spoke.

'Excellent. Excellent. Now tell me about our mutual friend Anthony. What does he look like?'

When she had done that, he asked her to describe Harold Wilson, Ted Heath and Anthony Wedgewood-Benn.

'Wonderful!' he said when she had finished. 'Your identi-kit pictures were almost perfect. Do you know that only one in ten reasonably intelligent adults can do that with any accuracy? Despite what television detective series tell you!' he laughed. 'You have an excellent memory, Sandra, but more than that your structural visualization is first rate.'

Sandra smiled.

'If you say so, love, but what's all this in aid of, if you don't mind me asking?' she said innocently.

'It's part of a course in observation. It's important for your work later. But now, I suggest lunch,' he said pleasantly.

They ate in a small French restaurant off Piccadilly Circus. Viktor did most of the talking, telling her about his life and family in Prague, showing her pictures of his children. He asked what sort of music she liked, whether she went to the theatre, and spoke intelligently about the plays then running in the West End. Not once did he mention the morning's training session. They could have been any couple having a quiet lunch and talking about old times.

But on the way back to her flat in his Jaguar, he mentioned the deal the STB was prepared to make her. Sandra agreed immediately, which surprised Viktor.

'Don't you want to know what you'll be doing?' he asked.
Sandra laughed.

'The same as usual, I suppose, dear. Using my body for the good of mankind.'

Viktor joined in her laughter.

'You could say that, I suppose. But even with your fine record, I don't think you'll be able to manage what we have in mind all on your own.'

They met again in Bayswater the following afternoon. Viktor had given her some 'homework' to do that morning. Following his instructions, Sandra had taken a bus from Park Lane to Kensington High Street. She walked to Harrods and strolled through the first floor, leaving out the Food Hall. Without taking notes, she was to describe to Viktor later 'anything unusual' she came across.

'There was a shoplifter I saw being nicked,' she told Viktor in the afternoon. 'Gosh, what a dirty little man he was! Scuffed shoes, an old grey coat and baggy trousers. And you'll never guess what he was trying to steal,' she giggled. 'Some Chanel perfume! Can you imagine, darling, what *he* would do with it. I felt sorry for him, but you've got to laugh.'

Viktor nodded.

'What time was this?'

'Eleven twenty, give a minute either way.'

'Very good. Your description is perfect, and the time is also correct.'

'How do you . . .' she started to ask, and then smiled at him. Of course, she thought. He had staged the whole thing. Either that, or she had been tailed all morning by someone who could verify her report. Either way, it did not matter. Sandra got the message. Her training was a serious business.

This was re-enforced over the next few weeks. Viktor expertly taught her the basic tradecraft of intelligence services common to every one from the CIA to the STB. He sharpened her already good memory by the use of mnemonics; trained her in cover behaviour – how to avoid showing

signs of guilt; 'eliciting information from unwitting inform-
ants,' as he called getting persons to reveal secrets without
asking them direct questions; and the basic elements of
secrecy – making sure that whatever she was seen to be doing
could in no way be linked to espionage work.

One day Sandra walked into the safe-house and flung her
handbag on the couch.

'I'm fed up with all this,' she said petulantly, slumping
down on the couch. 'I don't want to be a spy, Viktor, if this
is what it means.'

Viktor grunted, and studied her for a few moments.

'My dear, you have not even scratched the surface as far
as training to be a spy is concerned,' he said quietly, with
an edge of irritation to his voice. 'You are an agent. No more.
What you have been taught is simply to keep you out of
danger. To recognize traps by other security services. To
reach meeting places without being seen. What to do in an
emergency.' He paused and paced round the room.

Sandra sulked. She did not like being told off like a little
schoolgirl.

'I'll put it another way,' Viktor swung round to face her,
his eyes angry. 'You are being trained not to appear too professional. *That* would draw attention to yourself. And you,
of all people, should realize that professionalism can be as
undesirable in secret agents as it is in prostitutes.'

Sandra took the point. And seemed to immediately forget
it.

The following day she was told to enter the Queensway
Underground, off Bayswater Road, take the tube to Oxford
Circus, change to the Bakerloo Line, get off at Piccadilly
Circus and then leave the station after walking completely
round it, as if confused about which exit to take.

'You're going to be tailed,' Viktor told her. 'Lose him.
It doesn't matter where, just lose him. Once you're out of
Piccadilly take a cab to your flat.'

'Is that all?' she asked, blinking her eyes.

Viktor was not sure if she was joking or not.

'Not quite,' he said. 'You've to complete the exercise
without letting the tail know you've spotted him – if you do,

that is. And don't give him the impression that you're trying to shake him. Okay?'

Sandra nodded. She was looking forward to the 'mission' as she called it. It was certainly better than sitting in a stuffy room in Bayswater learning a load of theory, as far as she was concerned.

She travelled to Oxford Circus, peering at the other passengers, breaking the rule of normality in that alone.

'People do not look at one another in tubes. They stare ahead,' Viktor fumed when she told him later.

But this was not what caused him to hit her for the first time during their friendly relationship.

At Oxford Circus, she waited for a Bakerloo Line train, walking up and down the platform, glancing at everyone else.

The train pulled in. Sandra stepped inside. But just as the doors were closing she jumped back on to the platform. She had seen this trick on television. It worked there, and worked also for her.

A seedy-looking little man, clutching a battered brown brief-case, jumped back off also, and stared at her in embarrassment. He was her tail, a private detective who specialized in divorce cases – and looked it.

She repeated her on-off trick in Piccadilly, and convinced no one was following her by that time, caught a cab home. She was sure she had played the game to perfection.

'I saw him,' she burbled excitedly to Viktor when he phoned. 'And got rid of him. This agent thing's getting exciting, darling.'

There was silence at the other end for a few seconds.

'I'll meet you at Sam's in ten minutes,' he said flatly.

She caught a taxi to 'Sam's', the code name for the safe-house. She flounced in to the front room, her auburn hair bouncing, her eyes wide and a broad grin over her face.

'You fool! You incompetent idiot!' Viktor screamed as soon as she had sat down. His face was white with anger. Sandra was so surprised that she continued to smile.

Viktor took two large steps across the room, raised his

right hand, and slapped her hard across the face with the back of it.

'I told you yesterday,' he raged. 'Have you forgotten? Professionalism is as undesirable in spies and agents as it is in prostitutes.'

Sandra's cheek smarted and there were tears in her eyes. She hadn't been hit like that since the bad times before Chelsea. She did not say anything to Viktor. She knew she was in the wrong.

'If this had been a real operation instead of an exercise you would have blown it all,' he went on. 'Now listen. On top of all you've already learnt, this is probably the most important aspect to remember in your new work.' He sat opposite her, and his tone was softer when he spoke.

'It's vital that you should know if you're being watched at any time,' he said. 'And it's also important to be able to shake any tail if necessary. But at all times *act innocent*,' he emphasized. 'It's always better to submit to surveillance than to show you're aware of it, or use what *you* think is some professional trickery to get rid of it. That's how you turn light surveillance into heavy. And then we're all in trouble. And then you're – as I said before – on your own.'

'I'm sorry,' Sandra muttered. 'I didn't realize.'

Viktor nodded. He did not smile or console her in any way. He was impressing on her that it was not a game they were playing. And this time, she really did take the point.

'And while we're at it,' Viktor said, 'some more basic rules.'

Sandra glanced at him. Did he never stop? She had taken out a small mirror from her handbag and was dabbing at her eyes with a tissue.

'Go on,' she sighed. 'I'm listening.'

'The same principle of overt professionalism applies to your personal behaviour,' he said. 'Don't use double-talk on the phone. Code-names, yes. If you have something confidential to say use the phone only to arrange a face-to-face meeting to pass the information on.'

For the next hour he ran over the basic rules of espionage,

rules she had heard over the weeks, but now made sense in the light of practical experience. He told her not to put special locks on her door, which would show she was worried about security checks. 'But,' he added, 'there should never be any incriminating papers left in your flat in the first place.' He told her never to leave her flat just to make a phone call from a telephone box; he said she should never park her car far from a building she was visiting, on the theory she would hide the fact she was visiting the building from her tail. 'Television stuff,' Viktor called these tactics.

Finally, he stood up and walked to the window, looking down into the street. It was dusk and the rush-hour traffic was beginning to build up. Horns and revving engines could be heard from Bayswater Road.

'You see, Sandra,' he said softly, still looking into the street. 'The essence of espionage is this – you must integrate all your actions into your completely normal behaviour. This behaviour is dictated by factors which have nothing to do with the espionage mission itself,' he explained. 'You wouldn't normally jump on and off a train or park your car half-a-mile from a friend's house, and so on.'

Sandra chuckled.

'Of course not, love. I see what you mean.'

Viktor turned to her, smiling. The street lights shining into the darkened room made his hair seem golden and his six-foot frame looked broad and strong.

'But then,' he said 'we are not training you to be a spy, as I've already told you. The basic tradecraft is good discipline for any kind of secret work. Although,' he added, laughing lightly, 'your objective is exposure, the opposite of secrecy. But all paths to those objectives must be taken in secret.'

Sandra stared at him. The playboy image had been shattered during her first few days of training. He had shown himself to be a disciplinarian, almost humourless and totally dedicated to Communism. But she was still attracted to him, in the way a child is to a strict teacher. And she was convinced he liked her, although she constantly asked herself whether this was genuine, or an element of his bizarre technique of control and training.

For after every training session, he would take her to a small restaurant, and twice they went back to his luxurious bachelor flat in the Boltings, Chelsea. But not once did he show the slightest sexual interest in Sandra. A fact which disappointed her, she was honest enough to admit. Not for the first time in her life she fantasized about sex. She imagined Viktor and her lying naked on a pile of money, she face down, and he standing over her with an erection. He would sink down to his knees and pulling her up, enter from the rear. But just before his climax, he would withdraw and scatter his semen over the money. An exquisite insult to capitalism, she thought.

But it was all a dream. Even when Sandra would deliberately not wear panties and let Viktor see this, he still insisted on talking about his time in Russia training to be a spy, or his life in Czechoslovakia. So Sandra gave up, and concentrated on her own training.

She found out his feelings for the others at the Embassy. How he was devoted to his brother Mikhail, who was the top man in the STB's London station; how he idolized the Ambassador Dr Nikolai Rybalkov, whom he claimed was a 'father figure' to him; his healthy working relationship – 'no more,' he emphasized – with his case officer Simon Simenovsky.

'Before we arrived the old gang at the Embassy were a bunch of thugs and crooks,' he claimed. 'But after Ivanov's defection, the KGB moved in and brought some sense to our work, and overhauled the whole system.'

Sandra would listen to this patiently over lunch or at his flat, wondering when the real work would start. One day she sat for three hours in his flat while he praised the Russian system of training, a system he had himself gone through, ending it at Gaczyna, where a simulated English town had been set up for spies to train in the mannerisms and habits of the British.

'Yes, the Russian training is the best in the world,' he concluded. Sandra nodded. She was seated in a deep leather armchair. Viktor was pacing about the room, his favourite mannerism when talking intensely or enthusiastically.

He came across and leaned on the arm of Sandra's chair.

'But I'll tell you this, Sandra,' he said, dropping his voice. 'Although Russian training is marvellous, we Czechs are more intelligent as individuals. We can make more use of the training than the Russians do themselves.' He paused, smiling proudly. 'That's why *we* are asked to do all the sophisticated clandestine jobs – like the one you are involved in.'

'Yes, Viktor darling, I'm sure you're absolutely right. But when does this work start?'

'Ah, women, women,' he sighed with mock disgust. 'Always so impatient. You still need some more training.'

Sandra wrinkled her nose.

'Oh not more, surely. What's it for this time?'

'Your speciality.'

'Which is?'

'Feathermucking, as our American friends in the CIA call it.'

'*What*?' Sandra asked incredulously, her eyes wide and round.

'Feathermucking,' he repeated. 'Literally mucking up the feathers. In bed. Using your . . . er . . . natural talents for espionage.'

'I told you, sweetheart,' she laughed, flinging herself back in the chair. 'I knew I would end up on my back!' She pouted her lips, pretending to be disappointed. 'And I thought I was going to be the first female James Bond.'

Viktor laughed loudly.

'You are, my dear. But you'll be using sex like he used bullets.'

'Viktor,' she smiled mischievously, 'I've been doing that for years.'

For years, she thought. Ever since I came to this damned capital.

CHAPTER 4

Time has blurred my memory so I'm not sure how long
I stayed in Glasgow after my little scene with Uncle George.
But I knew I had to leave. There was nothing keeping me
there. The students at college bored me with their incessant
talk of sex, how they would change the world, and examina-
tions. In that order.

My mother and I seemed to live on different planes. Not
only would she not discuss my rapidly developing femininity
– I was a cup 34A at seventeen – but anything not connected
with cooking, sewing or the house brought a blank gaze to her
face and the comment, 'Young girls shouldn't be thinking
about such things. When you get married, you'll have plenty
to occupy your mind.'

'Such things' included what I was going to do with the
rest of my life; what it was all about anyway; and why did
my father have to die so young?

And she wondered later why she couldn't understand me!

There was one thing I had to do before leaving Glasgow.
Lose my virginity. Believe it or not, I was still 'intact'. And
having decided to go to London, which was then the swinging
capital of the world, it seemed fairly important at the time
that I was ready to join the swingers.

I chose Angus Sinclair to bestow on me the honour of
womanhood. He worked as a technician in the Natural
Philosophy Department of Glasgow University. I'd met him
in a café and liked him from the start. He was twenty-eight,
eleven years older than me, and had a mind the size of
Clapham Common as far as I was concerned.

When he spoke about Marx and left-wing alternatives
he did it with authority instead of the emotional rubbish I
was hearing at college. At least Angus had read the books –
which impressed me.

47

We saw each other a few times, progressing quickly from a good-night kiss to some heavy petting in his flat. I knew Angus had to be the one to initiate me into the mysteries of the body. But when it did happen, I was not ready!

It had been a normal night. The café, some cups of coffee, a couple of banana sandwiches or something equally esoteric – and a heated discussion about the Labour Party. On the way back to Angus's flat he suggested we bought a bottle of Mateus Rosé. Oh, dear, when I think about it! With hardly anything to eat, the small room filled with books and a bed, and me desperate to stay sober enough to have at least *some* control over the situation.

We finished the bottle and before I knew it, I had my denims around my ankles, my panties about my knees, and Angus wearing only a thick white woollen jumper, his shoes and socks and a lustful grin on top of me. It certainly wasn't the mystical experience D. H. Lawrence wrote about.

I felt some pain and then Angus stopped.

'You're not . . .' he said.

'I'm not now,' I told him.

'Oh God.'

'Oh God, what?'

'I didn't know. Are you all right? Did I hurt you?'

For the next half hour he wouldn't touch me. He sat in a chair opposite, while I still lay dripping small drops of blood on his carpet, waiting for him to take me to the moon.

He kept asking if I was feeling all right, and he didn't mean it to be like that and so on.

By the time he did come back I was feeling as sexy as a wet rag. All through his pushing and pulling he kept asking me if I hurt, was I going to be all right, how sorry he was. And then suddenly pulled out of me.

'I don't have any contraceptives!' he shouted, jumping up and pushing his rapidly dwindling penis back in his trousers, which he was tugging on.

It certainly was a great moment in my young, innocent life.

But at least I'd lost my virginity, even though I hadn't

had the universe-shattering orgasm I'd hoped for. I consoled myself with the thought that London's a big, swinging place, and I would hit the heights of sexual fulfilment there.

I went on a few marches in Glasgow, I can't remember what they were for now, but my heart wasn't in it. Once, during a march, I was sitting in George Square with sore feet. This bearded fellow beside me was desperately trying to convince me he had everything worked out.

'We get the youth of this country first,' he told me. 'Tell them what Mao said to the Chinese kids – the world belongs to you, he said. And once they realize that, then the Revolution'll take place.'

'I agree. Definitely. How do you tell them?'

'Through the youth movements, obviously. Me, I've got this job starting next month as a warden at a Youth Hostel in the Kyle of Lochalsh, across from Skye. I'll leave a few leaflets lying around, talk to the kids and get them organized. Put them in touch with their local activists,' he said. He was only a few inches away from my face and I can still remember the smell of garlic and onions coming from him as he spoke. I wondered if I should tell him, but decided it would be very bourgeois to do so.

'I'm not the only one,' he breathed. 'Go to the hostel in Kendal and ask for Tom Mason. He's the warden there, doing a grand job, he is, spreading the message. It's all planned, you know. It's all been worked out.'

'What happens when everyone gets the message?' I asked innocently.

He snorted. Really snorted.

'Its the Revolution, kid. It's the Revolution. And listen,' he said two inches away from my ear. 'On the first day of the Revolution, kid, I'm going to get a machine-gun and go into the streets and shoot every capitalist bastard I see.'

He was serious. And when I asked him how he would know which people were capitalists, he grinned.

'I'll know, kid. I'll know.'

I left for London the following week, if only to put as great a distance as possible between the bearded Communist Al Capone and myself. Mad days, I tell you. Mad days.

But nothing compared to London and Alec, the Notting Hill anarchist. But I'm going too fast again.

Can you imagine where I stayed when I first came to London? The YWCA! You see, my head was filled with hazy notions of revolution and doing something positive. Most of the people I knew in Glasgow sat around coffee shops or lay around their flats smoking pot and talking about the 'lousy system'. They weren't doing anything to help the oppressed masses they kept speaking about. I felt useless, wasted. I wanted to do something . . . something worthwhile. At least the YWCA would give me a fresh start.

Fresh isn't the word. I met more clean-living, clean-thinking girls than I'd seen all my life in Glasgow. They weren't a bad bunch I suppose, once you got used to the smell of Lifebuoy soap, their unmade-up faces, sensible clothes and shoes and the fact most of them carried bibles in their handbags.

At first, I wore denims, put on make-up and carried a packet of condoms in my handbag in case I was raped by all the London swingers I'd been told about. After Angus I was taking no chances! Of missing out, that is.

As it turned out, the swingers seemed to keep themselves to themselves, and I never came across them until much later on. When London was no longer the so-called Swinging Capital.

I had a little money my aunt had given me, convinced I was leaving Glasgow and all its 'benefits' because of my uncle.

But I still wasn't doing anything. I made a couple of friends, changed my style of clothes, and confided in them.

'Come along with us to the Salvation Army meetings,' they suggested. 'You'll do a lot of good work there.'

Good Work! Oh, at first it all seemed so sincere, so helpful. *Hallelujah*! I stood with them – uniform and everything – on the street corners, bashing a tambourine, handing out soup to the down-and-outs.

But after a month of this, my feet aching every night, and asking the *people*, the real people what they thought of God and Christ and Salvation and having them laugh in your face and tell you they'd say anything for a bowl of soup, my enthusiasm began to lag.

Okay, okay, I know that happens to everyone in an organization like the Sallies. But what happened to me next finished me forever as far as doing 'Good Work' was concerned.

I made the mistake – at the time it didn't seem so, of course – of confessing my waning faith to the leader of the group, a Major Alexander Johnson, an ex-sailor who had seen the light by realizing he was different from other sailors who only wanted to 'fornicate, fight and drink', as he put it.

Well, he took me back to his room behind the London Hospital in the East End. The walls were covered with crosses and pictures of Christ. He brought out a bottle of wine, mumbling about water being changed into wine. I think it was meant to be a joke. I didn't laugh. All that holiness surrounding me put me off.

We finished the bottle between us, and he told me his life story, how I had a long struggle ahead with the Devil if I wanted to rid myself of the doubts I was having and how my destiny had been all worked out by the Lord. I believed it! Even when he took his jacket off – he had red braces, I remember – and rested his head on my lap and started telling me how wonderful it was that the Lord had made men and women and what a joy there was to be had from this.

It's the wine, I kept telling myself. He's only trying to help you. But when he put his large, hairy hand on my knee, I had no doubts left.

The Bible-thumping, holier-than-thou Major was trying to get me to bed! I couldn't believe it! So this was where my 'Good Work' had got me.

I pushed him away and he landed flat on his back. He grovelled about the floor begging forgiveness. That was just too much. I turned my back on him and the whole Army. They were as corrupt as everyone else, I thought.

I slammed the door behind me and walked through the night until I finally caught a bus to the YWCA where I packed my clothes and headed for Notting Hill.

The only good thing to come out of my time in the Sallies was meeting a new group of people who used to hang about the East End and sometimes come down from Notting

Hill. They were the rebels without causes, the black militants, the white liberals and commies, the yellow revolutionaries and anyone who didn't fit. They used to hang about the Sallie Hall late at night drinking soup or sipping mugs of tea. They seemed to be able to get through to the down-and-outs more than we could with our God-Loves-You approach. They were filled with energy, life and expectation. And I loved them.

It was a coloured boy named Alec who made the greatest impression on me. He described himself as the only anarchist with a soul I would meet. I can still see his shining, smiling face, those big saucer eyes which made him look so innocent when he wanted. And even when discussing politics he had a twinkle in them that made it difficult to take him seriously. But he was bitter about the way the Establishment was running the country. He told me one night why. And he spoke in his deep, rich voice, his eyes did not sparkle, and I could feel the hate, the power behind his words. It still makes me shiver.

We were sitting in a corner of the hall, me in my uniform, Alec in his US Army combat jacket and denims.

'Look baby,' he said, looking me straight in the eyes. 'You know the system is crap. The system knows it's crap. But they can't see anything else. Any other alternatives. They don't talk *with* the people, they talk *to* the people. Tell them the system's great, they've never had it so good and all that bullshit. So they get the people working in factories, living in faceless boxes. And they persuade them to buy washing machines and fridges and fancy cookers and bigger televisions to put in these houses made by some other poor mother-fuckers in factories.

'The people are being brainwashed, baby, into thinking that God is a twenty-three-inch television screen and all life is there and they don't have to live it. Sit in your boxes and watch all life in comfort. And they believe that shit. And they go and work harder in their sweat-boxes of factories for bigger and better capitalist toys.

'You've seen the down-and-outs, the living sewer of humanity. Now go and meet the workers. The workers!

Ask any poor sod in a factory what he's been working for, what he's doing. He'll tell you it's for the wife, the kids, for a new car, for a holiday in fascist Spain or Portugal, and don't talk to him about the politics because he's only going for a sun-tan, and Christ, he's only going for two weeks on a package trip. What do you expect him to do, the brain-washed sucker'll say, start a revolution?

'So you see, baby, it's a brainwash operation. Get the working classes making goods for each other and you've got the system staying nice and safe. But Lenin said the capital-ists would destroy themselves. Bullshit! We gotta give the capitalists a kick in the ass. We gotta destroy the illusion. They want us to be employed making their fancy machines. We say no. What we're going to do is take your money, blow it and do fuck all. That's what we do. And so we take their money from Social Security. But we sure as hell don't feel social, and Christ, you think we feel secure?'

I didn't follow everything he said. I didn't have to. I *felt* what he was saying was right. And it was Alec who suggested I enrolled at night classes to study Marx, economics and other 'important subjects'. It was Alec who began to shape my jumbled thoughts about doing something worthwhile.

I used to look forward to our talks. I knew I could fall in love with him. A pure love, a genuine meeting of minds. It would have to be. Alec was a self-confessed homosexual.

So I headed straight for Alec's place that night after my run-in with Major Johnson. As it turned out, it was impossible to stay with him for two reasons. His bed-sit was too small. And he shared it with his boy-friend, a law student of all things, and they didn't like women around.

I moved around a lot then, from communes to squats to sharing floors. It was awful.

I had a room in a commune in Notting Hill for a while. Run by Jack Derby, who saw himself as an ageless student of the revolution, there were about twenty people in the old Victorian house at any one time. Jack, who was in his forties with a black straggly beard and deep-set grey eyes, was con-vinced there was a 'bourgeois plot' to dominate women, and the commune should not 'align itself to this false way of thinking'. In practice this meant every woman in the commune could sleep with the man of her choice, and *vice versa*.

I soon worked out that the rule was for Jack's benefit. He was, you see, the most over-sexed man I've ever met. If he didn't have a woman at least once a day, he would become grumpy and bad-tempered.

I didn't mind his conditions, still hoping to find my Great Experience. The trouble was the men in the commune took their sex as seriously as their Marx. They made love – if I can call it that – with all the seriousness of a judge delivering the death sentence.

I'll give you an example. I would be approached during the evening and told I was to be 'experienced' that night. If I said no, then I was a 'bourgeois sow', because I had not made my choice first, and then had the nerve to refuse!

We'd go up to his room and sit on the bed either drinking or smoking pot and *always* – I mean always, no matter who it was – have a ridiculous discussion about women being the tools of capitalism. Inevitably, the talk would end with the question, 'Do you now feel you can make love in a truly revolutionary spirit?'

I would nod and begin to undress. Of course, after about half an hour of deep political foreplay I was as sexed-up as a cold fish. No wonder I never had an orgasm! I was seriously beginning to wonder if sex was all people claimed.

In the same commune was a twenty-year-old called Robert with whom I used to dread going to bed. All through our love-making he wouldn't stop quoting Marx or Lenin. He had it down to a fine art. He would push into me shouting 'Abolition of the Family!' and withdraw screaming, 'The bourgeois sees his wife as a means of production!' His timing was immaculate. As he climaxed he would yell, 'Workers of world unite!' Which was how I knew that night's fantastic trip to the stars was over.

Oh yes, and there was Allen. He would pummel himself into me muttering, 'Fuck the middle classes. Fuck the ruling classes. Fuck the politicians'. I would lie there and wish he would stop thinking about the class structure and concentrate on me.

Oh, there were so many like that. So many fervent young men, so many passionate boys, so many desperate men that I've lost track of them all.

I was living on Social Security by this time, and pulling in a few pennies from selling the *Morning Star* outside factory gates, something I saw as having no relation to the class struggle at all. I decided I'd had enough of my house-hopping, bed-hopping existence when I discovered to my horror I'd caught VD.

I was shocked. I couldn't believe it! Me? It was impossible. Well-brought-up girls didn't catch that sort of thing. And when they asked me at the hospital did I have any idea who gave it to me, I had to shake my head. There were so many in those days! You can imagine how I felt when the doctor shook his head in disgust!

Luckily, it wasn't a serious dose, but enough to really scare me. I wanted a job, a nice flat and some respectability. Which I was able to get through Tom Courcey, thank heavens.

Tom was an underground journalist with *International Times*, and sometimes wrote for a leading music paper. I didn't like him at first. He used all the clichés of revolutionaries, unlike Alec, who was a revolutionary by nature.

He was fairly tall, but fat, and wore his hair in an Afro style which made him look ridiculous. He went around telling everyone he was a white man with a black soul. Alec called him the worst example of pretentiousness he'd ever met, and I agreed. 'But,' he said, 'he's useful. So we humour him, baby, we humour him.'

Which is exactly what I did.

Tom shared a flat in Chelsea with four other tuned-in journalists. This was their headquarters where they lay about all day, writing occasionally, smoking pot constantly and changing records on the hi-fi system. Their record collection was, to my mind, limited. It comprised solely of Bob Dylan albums.

Tom took a liking to me, and after making sure he was clean, I let him make love to me. It was like performing in the middle of a circus ring! People would burst in to his bedroom, shouting about a new political coup in Africa or waving a new underground paper. Tom didn't mind this and often stopped, leaving me lying there, to have a discussion about the latest piece of earth-shattering news.

But, as Alec had said, he was useful. I was offered a job on *IT*, covering demos up and down the country. The pay wasn't fantastic, but my living expenses were next to nothing as I was sharing a small flat in Holland Park with another girl. I took a shorthand and typing course which came in very useful later.

I was soon hitching around Britain meeting the leaders of various movements. But as I became more and more involved in these leftist activities, I began to discover they were all saying the same thing! I found myself time and time again asking myself what it was all about.

The thing is I agreed that the downtrodden masses – hospital workers, factory workers, so-called public servants like teachers and so on – *were* being used. I really wanted to do something about it. But had no idea what. My only hope was that all the movements would join up one day. But even I couldn't see *that* happening.

And the whole business with sex was also making me frustrated. Was there something wrong with me? My flat-mate, a typist with a car hire firm, would tell me how wonderful such-and-such a man had been, and weren't we lucky to be living in the Age of the Pill, and wasn't sex the greatest thing ever? I would nod, wondering where, oh where, was I going wrong?

And then I met Hath, who not only changed my ideas about sex, but a lot of other things as well. In fact, I can honestly say had it not been for that chance meeting one rainy afternoon in February, I would still be living in a small flat somewhere and all this business would never have taken place.

But let's take it step by step . . .

CHAPTER 5

It was the sort of day in Czechoslovakia that the monks of
the Knights of the Cross Monastery on the Moldau River
would have thanked God for creating. Not a cloud in the
hard November sky, and the huge cupola and handsomely
sculptured façade of the monastery gave an impression
of dignified serenity. The high vaulted corridors round the
rectangular courtyard were criss-crossed by black shadows
of pillars.

But no monks walked quietly under the Eucalyptus trees.
No chants were heard on this brittle winter's morning.
Two men, one carrying a brown folder under his arm, and
the other with his hands clasped behind his back, sauntered
round the courtyard, their heads bowed, talking quietly to
each other. One was Russian and the other, the man with the
folder, Czech.

They entered the domed chapel, thought by some to be
one of the finest examples of eighteenth-century restoration
in Eastern Europe. One of the walls was lined with medieval
paintings of saints, and as the sun filtered through the
stained-glass windows, these holy men seemed to be smiling.
This deliberate and brilliant trick of design was lost on the
two men. It was not a chapel they were entering. It was the
principal conference room of the STB, and the smell of
Turkish coffee had long since replaced that of incense.

'Well, comrade,' said the Russian when they were seated
at the large table, two small cups of thick, black coffee
between them. 'It looks as if Simenovsky was right. And if
these reports of Pavlenko's you've got there are correct,
Sandra Brown seems a most able pupil. Too able, perhaps.'

The other man chuckled.

57

'Always suspicious. One day you'll shoot your own reflection.'

The Russian smiled.

'That's why we'll always succeed. Taking nothing for granted. I don't like to remind you, but if it had not been for us, your London station would probably by now be run by the CIA and SIS men.'

'Ah, the bad old days! Times change, my friend, times change. No one denies the benefits your re-organization gave us. But we digress,' he said, smiling nervously and tapping the folder in front of him. 'The girl has only a few more weeks and some practical tests left before we are ready.'

The Russian nodded. On the surface the two men were friendly, but both knew who was the boss.

'We will need more funds,' the Czech went on. 'The Red Circle is going to cost more than originally anticipated. You've seen the figures, what do you think?'

'We agree. The money will be there when it's needed.'

'The whole one million pounds?'

'If it's needed, yes,' the Russian replied, his face showing no emotion. 'But we must see how this girl comes out of her practical tests. If she fails, Operation Red Circle is suspended indefinitely.'

'I don't think she will. I have faith in Viktor Pavlenko.'

'And Simenovsky?'

'Of course, of course. But he's only the case officer. That loveable rogue, his brother, Mikhail Pavlenko is in charge of the London station. He's no fool. He knows if Red Circle fails, he's finished as well.'

The Russian stood up.

'Good. We'll wait for the next reports,' he said. 'And now I think I'll go home and do some gardening. It's too nice a day to spend cooped up in this holy mausoleum.'

The Czech strolled with his KGB 'uncle' back through the courtyard. They were deep in discussion. Trying to decide whether or not it was better to plant an early crop of potatoes in December or February.

Sandra rang the bell of the Bayswater safe-house. Viktor came to the door, his face grim, and ushered her in. Was there something wrong, she wondered? Normally he greeted her with a smile, a light kiss on the cheek.

He swung round on her in the front room.

'You've been found out, Sandra. We know the truth.'

Sandra paled and her heart beat faster. What was he talking about? Her meeting with her friends in Notting Hill the week before? But she hadn't mentioned anything about her training to them. The fact she had just opened a private bank account in Switzerland to put aside money in case anything went wrong in this country?

'I . . . I . . . I'm not sure what you're talking about,' she stammered.

Viktor stared grimly at her for a few seconds. He started to smile and then burst out laughing.

'You see! It works! Say what I said to anyone, and they become worried. Everyone has a guilty conscience to some degree. Oh, I would love to know what went through your pretty head when I surprised you.'

Sandra slumped down on the couch.

'Very funny, darling,' she said flatly. 'What were you trying to prove?'

'One of the basic principles of your new speciality-feather-mucking.'

'Which is?' she asked, completely confused.

'*That everyone has a guilty conscience.* And it's that you must play on in your work for us,' he said. 'Put it this way. Your job will be, through sex, not to put any target into a blackmail position as such. It will be to find out about his personal life. His weaknesses, his areas of *guilt.*' He leaned forward, his eyes bright, his fair hair falling over his forehead. He brushed it back quickly. 'And it is on these areas of guilt we work.'

'Won't having sex with me be enough?' she asked.

'No, no, no,' he shook his head. 'Visits to prostitutes take place every day among the powerful and wealthy.' He paused. 'If the target, however, feels guilty about it himself, *then* we have something. One man's guilt is another man's joke. The Trappist monk who sees an exposed thigh passing his window can feel just as bad as a child molester.'

Viktor went on to discuss in general terms basic weaknesses of all human beings, sex being high on the list. Sandra, like a good student, sat with her arms folded, her brown eyes half closed, watching him. Only the hint of a smile on her perfectly made-up face gave her away. It was obvious Viktor was speaking about the theory of human frailty. She had had the experience.

But she let him go on, couching everything he said in psychiatric terms, speaking with a confidence as if he was the only one with such knowledge.

'Um, Viktor, love,' she finally said after he had spoken non-stop for half an hour. 'I agree with you. Most civilized human beings *are* weak-willed, self-centred and pander to their weaknesses if given half a chance.' She smiled sweetly, cocking her head to the side. 'But please, what has this to do with what I'll be doing!'

'Yes, yes, I'm coming to that,' he replied, obviously annoyed at being interrupted in the middle of what he considered to be a vital stage in Sandra's education. 'The point is, given a weakness, it's a man's own view of it we work on. We don't think of *what* he's done, be it masturbating in the gentlemen's toilet at King's Cross Station or raping a fifteen-year-old girl. We want to know how he sees it himself.' He paused and laughed. 'You know, there was a blackmailer who collected fortunes from a famous actress over the years by threatening to expose the fact that she had false teeth!'

Sandra laughed.

'That's like D . . . . . M . . . . ., the singer, who wears a chest wig! It fell off one night in bed. You should have seen his face!' she squealed. Her eyes were sparkling at the memory, the dimples on her cheeks deep as she laughed uncontrollably.

Viktor was caught up in the hilarity.

'Exactly,' he grinned. 'And the time those feathermuckers in New York took pictures of an Arab in bed with a parking lot attendant, a call-girl, and this is true, I swear, *a poodle!*'

Sandra's eyes widened.

'A poodle?' she repeated.

Viktor nodded, smiling broadly.

'The feathermuckers took them to his wife and told her they would cost a thousand dollars each,' he went on. 'She was delighted! She ordered six of each, planning to pass them round at a cocktail party, to amuse the guests. She quickly changed her tone, however, when the feathermuckers told her they were going to expose the fact that the parking lot attendant was black, the call-girl Jewish and the poodle French. That's when the blackmail pressure became effective,' he concluded.

'I take your point,' Sandra giggled.

'The only trouble with that sort of operation,' Viktor said seriously, 'is the whole thing had to be set up. It took time, and may not have come off in the end. The feathermuckers in question were not ours, they were from Mossad, the Israelis' secret service, and it was a bad operation from the word go. What I'm saying, Sandra, is this,' he said, leaning back and gazing at the ceiling. 'The best form of feathermucking operation is a retroactive one, or one in which you can threaten the mark with exposing something he has done in the past.'

Sandra nodded.

'Most of the people I know have something to hide.'

'Yes, but it's not that easy,' he said, still looking upwards. 'Retro operations are strange. For example, suppose you found out that I'd had a secret affair with a member of the aristocracy four years ago and my wife didn't have the slightest suspicion. So you would threaten to expose me. Useless,' he shook his head. 'I'd appear a Don Juan. Expose my past infidelities and people would see me as a romantic.' He looked at Sandra, his eyes laughing. 'And the same goes for any crooked dealings I may have done a few years ago. You know what they'd say? We feel sorry for him. Or, isn't he a wonderful man to have reformed the way he has?'

Sandra looked puzzled.

'So what's the point in going to all the trouble of getting him to bed in the first place?'

'Ah, don't forget we're talking about retro operations. You're right of course, what would be the point? But you're trying to find something out, remember. Also, and you know this better than me, once a man feels he has satisfied himself and a woman, he feels he can take on the world. He is invulnerable – he thinks.' He paused, looking at Sandra's smiling face.

'Go on,' she said, nodding.

'But,' he leaned over in front of her, 'you know that very few men *can* satisfy a woman or even themselves,' he smiled. 'And that's where your particular skills come in. Where the skills of every well-trained swallow come in.'

The rest of the afternoon was spent by Viktor outlining the various secret pasts which had been used successfully for retro operations. Sandra never took notes at the training sessions – 'No spy or agent worth tuppence keeps a journal,' Viktor had told her at the start of her training. And at each session, she was quizzed on the previous lesson.

There were only five basic situations that could be used in retro operations, Viktor claimed. Where a mark was not who he claimed to be, and was hiding his real identity; where a man had a false reputation – a hero who won a top medal because he was too scared to run, for example; when a man was in a bigamous situation and had another wife in another country, perhaps; where the mark had had a homosexual affair in the past and now had a 'macho' image – this was one of the most successful, Viktor told Sandra; and finally where the mark had been involved in a crime involving moral turpitude, like incest or acting as a church warden and stealing part of the collection.

'There's only one common denominator, if you look at it objectively,' he ended up. 'And that's moral turpitude, a feeling of having sinned in something that involves either sex or cheating.'

Sandra sighed. The training sessions had been going on for almost two months without a break. She was, quite simply, becoming bored and wondered when it would all end. She could see that there was a pattern to the whole thing – the basic tradecraft followed by specialist feathermucking instruction.

But it all seemed so easy, so straightforward. So simple.

in fact, that Sandra felt more than ready to start her new work for the STB. Suddenly one morning she was jolted out of her complacency.

It was 10 am and she was resting in bed after a late night when the intercom buzzed. Sleepily, pushing her hair back, she lifted the phone, her eyes closed.

'Yes? Who is it?'

'Police, Miss Duvalle. 'We're doing a house-to-house check. There's been a large robbery near here.'

'I don't know anything about any robberies,' she mumbled.

'We have to ask you some questions. Routine.'

Wearily, she pressed the door connection, and a few minutes later, wearing only a silk gown, she opened the door to two tall men.

'We're sorry to disturb you, but it is important,' one of them said.

When they were seated in the lounge, Sandra blinking herself awake, one of them took out a notebook.

'There has been no robbery, Miss Duvalle. We're from the Special Branch and want to know your connection with the Czech Embassy.'

Sandra yawned.

'I'm sorry, I've had a long night,' she said. 'The what? The Czech Embassy? I don't know anything about it.'

'We have reason to believe you have been seeing a Viktor Pavlenko. Is this so?' They asked the questions in turn, as if having agreed before. This irritated Sandra, but she kept calm.

'I've never heard of him. Oh, wait a minute, I have. Isn't he the playboy who owns a travel agency? I've seen him at cocktail parties, but never spoken to him,' she added innocently.

For three-quarters of an hour they grilled her about Viktor and the Czechs and tried to get her to admit she was in contact with the STB. Sandra kept up her act of ignorance.

Finally, the men shrugged and stood up.

Sandra jumped up to see them to the door, her heart thumping with the strain of the pretence. And then suddenly, the men began to laugh.

'Congratulations, Miss Brown,' one said, using her real name. 'Viktor sent us,' and he pulled out a card which she could not understand anyway. 'A little test in interrogation. You came through very well.'

Sandra laughed also, a mixture of relief and pleasure.

They turned to the door. One of them turned back casually and looked down at Sandra, smiling.

'Where was it you did your training? Bayswater or Hampstead? Viktor told me, but I've forgotten. It might be the same as my location.'

'Bayswater,' she smiled. 'It was . . .'

She didn't see his hand come up, but she felt it. It hit her across the mouth and she was flung across the room, hitting the opposite wall, sliding to the floor in shock and pain. She tasted the blood from her split lip.

The men stood over her, their faces hard.

'I could have been a genuine SB officer,' the one who had hit her said. 'Never trust anyone, you hear? Never relax for a moment, even when you think you're safe.'

Sandra was sobbing with fright. Neither of the men made a move to help her as she struggled to her feet, not caring about her gown which had slipped open, showing her nakedness. She stumbled into her bedroom and collapsed on the bed, staining the white silk sheets with her blood. A few minutes later she heard the front door slam.

The following morning Viktor never mentioned the incident. Neither did she. She had learnt the lesson well.

About eleven o'clock Simenovsky appeared.

'The training's over,' he said. 'Now I'll give you an oral examination,' he added tersely.

Sandra settled back in one of the armchairs and lit a cigarette, crossing her legs to make sure Simenovsky had a good view of her thighs.

He pretended not to notice, but Sandra could not help smiling when she saw, during the next hour of questioning, his eyes dart quickly down to her legs, and back again to her face.

'Now, Miss Sandra,' he began, 'what would you do if one

of your marks insisted on telling you about a secret formula his office was working on?'

'I'd say I didn't understand all those technical things but admired men who did.' She had put on a soft voice when answering. 'I'd say it just like that,' she added.

Simenovsky nodded.

'Good. Very good. But why? Isn't the job of an agent to find out secret information?

'Uh-uh,' Sandra shook her head. 'That's *your* job, not mine darling,' she smiled. 'I'm only interested in his personal life. And as far as he tells it. Even if he *wanted* me to know about the X-45 ultra-sonic homing device I'd show no interest at all.'

'Excellent,' Simenovsky commented. 'And suppose he asked you to have oral sex, would you refuse?'

Sandra chuckled.

'At first, yes.' She hesitated before going on, lightly licking her lips. The effect was not lost on Simenovsky or Viktor who both shifted their positions noticeably. 'But then I would let him talk me into it. Because even though I might not want to do it, I want the mark to get the impression he's dragging me down to his level, make him feel he's sharing his base wickedness with me. Make him more vulnerable, in other words.'

Simenovsky was genuinely impressed. Sandra answered every question perfectly. Finally the case officer looked across at Viktor.

'Congratulations, Viktor,' he said, beaming. 'You've got an intelligent young lady here. You've done your job well. And now, by way of a celebration, I will take you both to lunch. Before the real work starts,' he added, glancing at Sandra.

The 'celebration' was held in the revolving tourist trap on top of the Post Office Tower, chosen by Simenovsky 'because there's not the slightest chance any of the three of us will run into someone we know'. They had smoked salmon, steaks, green salads and it being 'an occasion' Simenovsky ordered champagne – the cheapest on the menu. Over coffee and liqueurs – brandy for the men, Cointreau for Sandra – Simenovsky leaned forward and lowered his voice so as not to be overheard by the serious American tourists at the next table.

'Your first job is by way of an ice-breaking operation,' he explained. 'It's to drop someone you know.'

Sandra showed no surprise. Viktor *had* done his job well.

'The mark's Lord Mallette,' Simenovsky went on, practically whispering. 'Freddy Mallette. He's a big fish. You know his reputation, Sandra, don't you?'

Sandra nodded. Freddy Mallette was considered to be an English gentleman of the old school. She had met him several times through their mutual friends, Sir Robert ('Bobby') and Lady (Debbie) Alspeth. Mallette was on a dozen corporate boards, and countless institutional ones, though his standing in the community depended more on his reputation for integrity and moral purity than for his brains.

'He's big, all right,' Sandra said. 'But what makes you sure he'll bite?'

Simenovsky grinned.

'He's been in the net. His name has appeared three times in the catalogue. Once for being seen as part of a "moral team" raiding a porn shop, where he showed a keen interest in the books with pictures of young girls; again for going in to a cinema in Soho with another moral team to see *I was a Teenage Nymphomaniac* or something like that; and thirdly for yet another raid on a porn shop where he actually stole some books on adolescent sex.'

'Old Freddy!' Sandra smiled, her eyes bright with amusement. 'Imagine him being into that sort of thing.'

'Quite, quite,' grinned Simenovsky. 'He's an important man as far as we're concerned. You can read the notes at the safe-house, but the fact you already know him makes you the obvious choice for the drop.'

And so as Sandra watched London circling past from the revolving madness that was the Post Office's and Billy Butlin's pride and joy, she was assigned her first espionage job.

And she was relieved. The waiting was over. It had taken her nearly eight years to have that feeling. At last she was doing something positive. Something worthwhile.

The notes told her very little. Mallette and some 'decency freaks' had been raiding a Soho porn shop, and the manager, a homosexual called Dicey, saw him pocket a book with explicit pictures of sex between old men and young girls. After they had left, Dicey did a quick tour of other porn shops and the managers of them recognized Dicey's description immediately, adding that Mallette always took an interest in the shelves with books about teenage sex.

Dicey knew he was on to something. He phoned Simenovsky at the Embassy and Mallette's name and photograph, taken from a newspaper clipping, were entered in the catalogue. Simenovsky was so pleased, he gave Dicey ten pounds – a fact entered in the notes.

The other stories were basically the same. Mallette, always on the pretext of investigating porn in London, would visit cinemas and bookshops. Sandra had been instructed to do nothing until Simenovsky had seen her the day following their lunch.

They met at the Hilton Coffee Bar and after coffee Simenovsky took her to a club in Halkins Street, which acted as a front for the STB. Sandra was not impressed with the lay-out of the club and said so.

'I know, my dear,' Simenovsky agreed. 'We inherited this from the old gang. It has only limited facilities for our work – but enough, I think.'

Sandra looked at him and frowned. She was beginning to wonder just how much the STB *did* know about the world of prostitution, despite Viktor's glowing remarks about them being smarter than the Russians.

The manageress of the club, 'Granny', was the third since the lay-out had been changed by Viktor's brother from a New Orleans whorehouse to a rustic cabin design, giving what Simenovsky called 'a comfortable, respectable feeling of intimacy'. Granny was a small, rather fat, extrovert lady with sagging breasts. She flung her arms round Simenovsky when she saw him and seemed to take to Sandra after being introduced.

'One can tell you've got breeding,' she said.

Sandra smiled politely.

The other two girls in the club looked at Sandra suspiciously, and only nodded when Granny introduced them before taking Sandra on a tour of the club.

'It's been set up like this on purpose,' she said. 'It's ideal for feathermucking in the same way *Playboy* magazine is ideal for the man of elegance and reputation who wants some erotica along with his Norman Mailer. They can relax and pretend they're only here for company and conversation.'

Sandra did not say much during the tour. As far as she was concerned, the club was as erotic as the emergency waiting room at the London Hospital. Everything was wrong about it, she thought. The booths were too large, the dance floor too large, the bar too small and the lighting amateurish. And the location was hopeless.

They ended in Granny's office, where Simenovsky was waiting. The two seemed to have a special relationship, a fact that Sandra was quick to notice. Simenovsky laughed a lot, and he and Granny touched each other often. There was some initial argument as to how Sandra should get Mallette into the club, during which time Sandra sat primly on a hard-backed chair listening to the plan unfold.

They finally decided that Sandra should meet Freddy socially, and take it from there. The plan was vague. Sandra immediately saw some flaws in it, but kept quiet. She would make her own improvements. She might not know everything about espionage, she thought, but when it came to sex and dealing with men, then she did not need much tuition.

The meeting with Mallette was easily arranged. She simply looked up his business number in the telephone book, re-introduced herself, reminding him that they had met at the Alspeths' cocktail parties, and wondered if she could see him to follow up the 'fascinating discussion' they had been having at the party.

Mallette vaguely remembered her and agreed to a meeting. Sandra suggested lunch at Claridges and they arranged to meet the following Friday, in three days.

At ten o'clock on the morning of the lunch Sandra went to the hairdressers. She had her page-boy cut washed out, her hair parted down the centre, and small ribbons put in each bunch over her ears. Back in her flat, she changed out of her slim-look trouser suit and put on a white blouse and full grey skirt which came to just below her knees. She creamed her make-up off and put a little rouge on her cheeks. She slipped on a pair of brown, flat shoes.

She stood in front of a full-length mirror on the wardrobe which housed her whips, costumes and sex aids. The irony was not lost on her, and she smiled. She looked nearly ten years younger, about eighteen or nineteen. Exactly what she wanted.

Then she went to meet her first target.

Mallette was already in the bar waiting. In his fifties, he was a stockily-built man, with broad shoulders, a square face with bushy eyebrows and deep-set grey-green eyes. At five foot six, he was about two inches taller than Sandra and was, as usual, dressed immaculately, wearing a Harris Tweed three-piece suit.

'Freddy, how are you?' Sandra asked in a clear, soft, almost childlike voice as she approached him with outstretched hand.

'Fine, my dear, fine. And how are you, Rochelle?'*

They chatted amiably for about ten minutes, talking of common friends and what each had been doing since they last met. Sandra's cover for social occasions was that she was a computer programmer which accounted for her strange hours. She told Freddy she had the day off, and so had plenty of time.

During their chat, Freddie drank scotch and soda. Sandra had tonic water.

'Drink does funny things to me at lunch-time,' she said in

---

* The name Rochelle will be used throughout on occasions when she was known as this.

a quiet apologetic voice, lowering her eyes as she did.

Freddy laughed.

'You young girls are all the same,' he said. 'Can't wait to get to the bright lights, and when you do, you can't take it!'

Over lunch Sandra insisted on only having a small glass of white wine for the same reason. They continued to talk about nothing in particular over the consommé, and it was only as they finished the Boeuf Wellington that Sandra pushed her plate away and put her elbows on the table, leaning her chin in her cupped hands.

'You know, Freddy dear,' she said, her eyes wide and staring directly at him. 'I really *was* impressed at the Alspeths' cocktail party with what you were saying about your work with the commission investigating . . . investigating,' she stammered, swallowed and looked down at the table, 'investigating pornography,' she said quickly, acting embarrassed at having even said the word.

'Was I talking about that?' he asked. Like most men full of their own importance he could not remember what he was saying from one day to the next. Something Sandra had already worked out for herself.

She nodded and looked up at him.

'I think it's wonderful. It must be a marvellous feeling knowing you are doing something to make the country a cleaner place to live in.'

'It is, my dear, it is,' Freddy smiled, looking into her eyes, and then glancing at her blouse and hair. 'It's terrible, this free rein the pornographers have. They've got to be stopped. You know you can't walk through the centre of London now without coming across some poster for a salacious film? Within one square mile of Piccadilly Circus there are at least thirty cinemas, not including private clubs, which show filth constantly.'

Sandra shook her head.

'It's awful,' she sighed. 'But at least you're doing something to help stamp it out,' she added earnestly. 'I wish I could help too. I feel so . . . so helpless in the face of it all.'

He leaned over and put his hand on her wrist.

'You're not to worry, Rochelle,' he said softly. 'I find it very heartening to meet young people like you who have not succumbed to the filth that's being spread . . .'

'But I want to *help*,' Sandra pleaded, sniffing with frustration. 'I want to help stop it.'

Mallette shrugged.

'I don't think you can help the Commission. The members are chosen by the Chairman, you see,' he said and paused. 'But there is an organization which I happen to be treasurer of, which is against the increase of permissiveness. Why don't you come along to some of the meetings?'

'What a super idea!' she said, sitting back and clapping her hands. 'I'd love to. Oh, Freddy, thank you. I didn't know such groups existed.' Her eyes were wide with excitement.

He beamed at her, like an uncle who has just given a favourite niece a birthday surprise.

After lunch, they waited outside as the commissionaire hailed a taxi. When the cab drew up, Sandra said she was only walking round the corner to Regent Street, in the opposite direction from Freddy. But just before he stepped into the cab, she stood on her toes, leaned across and kissed him lightly on the cheek.

'Thank you, Freddy darling, for an absolutely divine lunch. I'll phone you tomorrow about these meetings.'

She stood watching the cab pull away, waving at him, a smile of happiness on her face.

The bigger the fish, she was thinking as Freddy waved back, the bigger they bite . . .

For the next three weeks, Sandra attended at least one anti-porn meeting a week. She applauded when various speakers talked about 'Sin stalking the land', or 'The total degradation of women for the pleasure and profit of a few men'. She frowned and nodded when someone stood up to speak about the 'Evil of Prostitution'.

Freddy Mallette was at all the meetings and they would meet later for a few words. Twice he ran her home. Twice she kissed him on the cheek. At the beginning of the third week, she phoned his office and arranged another lunch.

This time they met at the Coq d'Or where Sandra insisted on having a salad. 'I'm going through a vegetarian spell,' she said. She was wearing a simple cotton dress, a white cardigan and white boots. Her hair, as ever, was parted, but this time pleated.

They spoke of the anti-porn meetings, and how worthwhile Sandra found it all. It wasn't until coffee – with brandy for Freddy, on its own for Sandra – that she fell silent.

'Is there something wrong, dear?' Freddy asked.

She shook her head.

'Sorry, I was thinking.'

'What about? Or am I being nosy?' he smiled.

'No, no,' she replied quietly. 'It's just . . . it's just . . . oh no, it's stupid,' she said shaking her head and smiling.

'Now you've got me interested. Do you have a problem? Can I help in any way?'

'It's not a real problem,' Sandra stared into her coffee cup as she spoke. 'And you'll only laugh if I tell you.'

'Try me.'

She curled one plait of hair around her fingers, before looking up.

'Well, it's got to do with these meetings we go to,' she said, her face troubled. 'I listen to everything that's being said, and agree with it. But do you know what I thought yesterday? I thought . . . no, it's terrible, I'm not telling you.'

'Now come on, Rochelle,' Freddy said, brusquely. 'I'm not letting you go until you tell me. You can confide in old Freddy Mallette, you know.'

She smiled gently at him.

'You are a dear,' she said. 'Okay. It suddenly struck me that I've never ever been to see one of those films that you and the others talk about. And I feel such a *hypocrite*, if you see what I mean. I said you would laugh at me, and you are,' she pouted when she saw Mallette smiling.

'Oh no, I'm not laughing, believe me,' he said. 'I hope you don't mind me saying this, but your naïvety is like a breath of fresh air on a summer's day. You're so sincere about everything, so intense. It does an old man good, I tell you. That's why I was smiling.'

'Oh, Freddy, love! You're not old,' Sandra teased.

'Well, you know what I mean. Compared to you I am. But you're right. I have to visit these dens of porn for the Commission – one of the more distasteful aspects of the job, I can assure you.'

Sandra leaned forward and clasped one of Mallette's broad hands between her palms.

'Freddy, darling,' she said breathlessly. 'Do you think you could take me along next time you go? As I say, I've never seen a *blue* film. And it would deepen my understanding of what we're fighting. I mean, Freddy love, I can't very well go on my own, can I?' She squeezed his hand. 'And you're so respectable and well-known. No one would think I actually *wanted* to see such a film.'

'You're a funny little thing, aren't you?' he said pressing her hand. 'Very well. I'm doing a swoop next week on that place at Piccadilly Circus. You can come with me then.'

Sandra smiled in appreciation.

'I can't wait,' she said honestly.

With Christmas only a fortnight away, Sandra was kept busy over the following few days as her regular clients all tried to see her before spending the holiday with their families. She had called Freddy at the beginning of the week when he told her he would be visiting the Jaxon Cinema on the Wednesday, and could she get away? She said she would re-arrange her shifts at the computer centre and meet him outside.

When she did turn up, wearing the same outfit as when they first had lunch, she was exhausted after being up until four every morning, doing what she called her 'full-time job'. But she was not too exhausted to pretend to be shocked by what she saw on the screen, which was in fact a very mild movie about a sixteen-year-old Swedish *au pair* working for two bachelor sons of millionaires.

And she was not too tired to grab Mallette's hand when an 'explicit', that is blurred, sex scene was shown. And if she had let her hand slip down to his thigh, then surely that was because she was stunned by the goings-on being played out on the screen? And if she felt Freddy's erection as he watched the simulated celluloid bed-games, then she gave no indication of it. And when she crossed her legs, letting her skirt ride up her thighs, just past her stocking tops, then surely this was because the seats in such cinemas were so uncomfortable, being made for men being more interested in their fantasies than their comfort? And surely Freddy was not sneaking glances down at her legs and thighs during periods of dialogue on the screen?

Of course he was, Sandra noticed with satisfaction.

The film over, Sandra thanked Freddy for a 'most interesting and educational afternoon'. One movie led to another, and soon she was accompanying him into the private clubs in Soho, where uncut, hard porn was shown. The hand on the thigh progressed to his crotch, where she would gently rub against his penis.

'It's awful to admit, I know,' she whispered when she first did this, 'but I do find some of the scenes very exciting.'

Mallette grunted.

Sandra soon realized most of their trips to cinemas had nothing to do with Freddy's work for the Commission. But she encouraged them, not openly, but by showing a keen interest in Freddy's so-called 'aims'.

What she was in fact doing was increasing Mallette's hypocrisy ratio. Freddy Mallette, the man thought to be fighting porn, considered to be above the gross temptation of sex, was the same man who was visiting porn cinemas at least once a week and being masturbated by a 'young' girl. If exposed, his hypocrisy would be seen to be enormous.

It was Sandra's first attempt at the game. And so far, according to Simenovsky, she was winning every move.

Christmas came and went. Mallette sent her a gold necklace as a 'little gift'. Sandra put it in her wall safe, along with the other trinkets she had collected over the years.

In mid-January, she met Mallette again at Claridges.

'Freddy, darling,' she said after a superb meal, 'you've been so kind to me over the past few weeks, and I've been telling my friends what a super man you are that they're all dying to meet you.'

Mallette grinned. Like most men with limited intelligence

74

he needed constant reassurance.

'That's damn nice of you, Rochelle,' he said. 'But you know what my time schedule is like.'

'Oh, you just have to pop into a little club we go to where we have coffee and discuss things. It's run by an ex-Guide captain who makes sure we young ladies don't get into trouble!' she laughed.

'A sort of youth club, you mean?' Freddy asked, having latched on to Sandra's deliberate phrase 'young girls' which she had emphasized.

'Yes, love. A youth club. It's in Halkins Street,' she said. 'Oh, do say you'll come along! They'll be so thrilled.' Sandra clasped her hands together. Her hair that day was tied in a bun at the back, emphasizing her oval face and large eyes. She smiled pleadingly at him, her dimples prominent on her unmade-up cheeks.

'Ooh, you girls! Very well, my dear. When?'

'Tomorrow night? That way you won't have to interrupt your working day.'

Mallette nodded.

'Good idea. Tomorrow night.'

Sandra then described some of the girls to Mallette, telling him that most of them had come down from the provinces like her and that Granny – 'We call her that because she's so sweet and kind' – looked after them until they could get settled. Mallette's interest was growing by the minute. Sandra was sure if the Prime Minister wanted to see Freddy the next night, Mallette would have made some excuse not to turn up.

After lunch Sandra went straight to the club. She put Granny in the picture as far as the cover story was concerned.

'We'll have to make some alterations,' Granny commented looking round the dimly-lit room.

'Have you time?'

'Wait and see,' Granny chuckled.

Sandra was waiting outside her flat the next evening when Mallette arrived to pick her up. She did not want his Lordship to see her apartment. No computer programmer could possibly afford the luxury she was living in. The cover she used for staying in the area was that she was living with a distant cousin, which explained why Freddy could not come up for coffee and drinks on the evenings he ran her home.

When they arrived at the club, Sandra was impressed. Gone were the dim lights and in their place were floodlights on tracks attached to the ceiling. The partitions between the booths had been removed and the tables stood close together. Checked cotton covers replaced the white table-cloths and the bar had had every drink removed from behind it. A milk cooler and rows of Coca-Colas stood in place of the bottles of spirits. A juke box in the corner played pop music, but not too loudly.

Sandra even had difficulty in recognizing the girls. No slinky silk dresses that night; no low-cut blouses with push-up bras; no make-up either and certainly no cigarettes, a large NO SMOKING sign reminding them of the rule. Instead, the girls wore simple frocks or jumpers and skirts, drank milk out of tall glasses or sipped their Cokes through straws.

It was, to all appearances, a well-run, orderly club for young people. There were even a couple of clean-cut, smartly dressed young men who looked as if they had just stepped out of Bible Class. In fact they were 'ravens', young homosexuals used for sexual blackmail, as Sandra found out later.

But as far as she was concerned, Granny herself was the *pièce de résistance*. Wearing a loose-fitting black dress that looked as if it had been bought at a jumble sale and with her grey hair tied in a top-knot, she blustered about like a mother hen protecting its brood.

'*Lord Mallette*!' she flustered when Sandra introduced her. 'Oh my goodness me! I can't believe it! Imagine, girls,' she said turning to the tables. 'It's Lord Mallette! Coming to our little club!' She took his hand and pumped it. 'We've heard so much about you from Rochelle. About your fine work in upholding the morals of this country.'

Mallette muttered his thanks.

'You could say we're in the same business, Lord Mallette,' Granny went on. 'In my own small, very small, way I'm

76

trying to stop my girls getting caught in the trap of wicked-ness.

'And an excellent job you're doing as well,' Mallette said, finally pulling his hand away.

Granny took him on a tour of the club. The office section and the small cinema used for showing blue movies to targets had been blanked off. But she did show him a bedroom with two large beds in it. Clothes lay scattered around the room, and a few suitcases were piled against the wall. Posters of Cliff Richard, Billy Graham and the Crucifixion Scene were pinned over the beds.

'Some of the girls, poor things, come down to London with nowhere to stay. I put them up here for a little while,' she explained, shaking her head.

Sandra waited at the bar, drinking coffee. When Granny and Mallette joined her, they were laughing and joking like the best of friends. They had some coffee and then Granny went over to a corner where an old battered desk stood.

'My office,' she shrugged apologetically.

Rummaging in the drawers, she pulled out a photo album.

'Our family album,' she smiled as she brought it across. 'Some of the girls we've had stay here in the past,' she added, flicking the book open. Badly taken snapshots were glued to the pages. 'I take all the pictures myself just to keep a record. You never know, some of the girls may come back one day and want to know what they were like when they first came to London.'

Mallette smiled politely as he looked at the photographs.

'And we must have one of you, Lord Mallette, with my girls. What a fine thing to show visitors!' she said and went back to her desk and found a cheap plastic Kodak camera.

'Now come along, girls. I'm going to take another picture,' she shouted, looking around. 'Now where? Ah, yes. Beside the juke box on the bench seat. That would be nice. Oh, I need a flash,' she said, putting her hand to her mouth.

Fumbling about the drawers, she found a small cube flash which she attached to the top of the camera.

'Now, girls, let Lord Mallette sit in the centre and you

gather round looking at him.' They followed Granny's instructions. Sandra at the end, her head turned to the side, smiling at Mallette.

Granny's flash popped, and she changed it for another. She took six photographs, two of them with a girl sitting on Mallette's knee.

'Thank you, Lord Mallette,' Granny finally said, putting the camera back in the desk. 'That was marvellous.'

Mallette stayed on for half an hour, talking to the girls and Granny. He was so impressed with the place, he insisted on writing out a cheque for £100 to contribute to the running of the club.

As he left he waved, and as Granny saw him to the door he said, 'And don't forget to send me one of the photographs.'

Granny smiled.

'Oh, you'll see them, Lord Mallette. I give my word.'

Back in the club, Granny opened a cupboard behind the bar and pulled out a bottle of whisky and a packet of cigarettes.

'Well done, girls,' she said. 'That was perfect.'

'What about the photographs?' Sandra asked. 'Did we act all right?'

'Marvellously,' Granny grinned.

For the cheap camera was in fact only camouflage. Inside was a miniature Minox camera which produced colour transparencies. It had been loaded with a special light-sensitive film, in case Mallette had decided *not* to sit near the juke box which was placed directly under a rack of floodlights above. Granny's flash was totally redundant, and by pressing a black panel at the back of the dummy camera, she operated the Minox. Instead of the six photographs Mallette thought she had taken, a complete roll of thirty-six had been exposed.

And when Granny told the girls to look at Mallette while he grinned at the camera, they did so in a way which would make it impossible to identify them later. And Mallette could not have known that the girls on either side of him had hitched up their skirts to show their stockinged thighs.

And he certainly had no way of knowing that the girl who sat on his knee was the same build and height as a young call-girl well-known to Scotland Yard. And a photograph of this girl would be taken at a later date after studying Granny's picture, and the young prostitute would sit on a man's knee in the same position. After which the darkroom technicians would begin working on both transparencies. The end result would be a photograph of Lord Freddy Mallette with a young call-girl sitting on his knee, surrounded by fawning girls who seemed to be wearing very short dresses.

It had been a good night. Sandra was delighted. As she changed into an evening dress to go off and meet John Baker, the industrialist, and one of Sandra's regular clients, she ran over the next few stages of Mallette's drop in her mind.

A few more visits to the club, get him to know some of the girls, and then the final set-up. Her fish would then be well and truly caught.

Sandra stood in a small room next to the bedroom in the club, and watched the two men in front of her arguing.

'How many times do I have to tell you?' one was shouting at the other, waving his hands in the air. He had on a bright red shirt, tight cord trousers and a blue silk scarf tied loosely around his neck. He was a homosexual.

'And how many times do I have to tell *you*?' the other screamed back. He wore a bottle-green, tight, ribbed polo neck jumper, fawn trousers and white shoes. He, too, was homosexual.

'A wide-angle lens won't work in here!' the first yelled. 'It'll distort the images. You're too close to the subjects.'

'Balls! How many photos have I taken?' the other asked, his hands on his hips. 'Go on. Tell me. You can't. Thousands, that's how many.'

'With a Mamiya or a Nikon!'

'A Nikon. But a camera's a camera.'

'No, it's not,' the first one leered. 'See what you know! A

Nikon close up'll take these shots A Mamiya won't.'

The other breathed in deeply and looked as if he was about to cry.

'Well, do it yourself, then, smarty-pants!' he huffed and flounced out of the room.

The man left in the room stood still for a moment and then rushed after his friend.

'John, John, love. I didn't mean it. Come back, please.'

Sandra shook her head. It was a madhouse. The club was filled with technicians, ninety per cent of whom seemed to be homosexual.

'They're safer to work with, dear,' Granny had explained. 'We've got something on them all so they do as they're told. We try to use homosexuals as often as we can. And,' she lowered her voice, 'they're such good workers! Just like women.'

Sandra laughed and wandered off to watch the preparations.

The bedroom still looked basically the same. The posters were in the same position over the beds. The Crucifixion Scene in the centre, flanked by Billy Graham and Cliff Richard. But the beds had been moved together, meaning that Christ looked straight down the middle of what was now one large bed. The fact that the holy picture was mounted on hardboard was no accident. The room in which Sandra had watched the argument was directly behind the print. At the right moment, Christ's head would slide to the side and a camera would be operated from the small room.*

To hide the sound of the camera clicking, a cheap stereo system had been put in the bedroom – 'a gift from a grateful past resident', should Mallette ask – and if that should fail, for any reason, the juke box had been moved closer to the door of the bedroom.

And if for any reason the lights were switched off in the bedroom, then the technician would use black photography. Special infra-red light would be beamed into the room

* Methods have now become much more sophisticated with the use of miniature TV cameras which can be operated from another room and video-taped. But this was during the early 1970s.

through a ventilation grille on the wall opposite the bed, and using treated film the camera operator would be able to produce passable if not first-class results.

The room was also bugged. An electronic expert placed the tiny transmitter in various places, testing it each time. He finally decided to put it in a box of sanitary towels on the assumption that even if Mallette became suspicious and began looking around he wouldn't look inside a box of tampons. If he should, however, he would see nothing except what he expected. The mike was slipped down the front of the box, taped into place, and the tampons put back in.

After about six hours of setting up, the club was finally ready for the drop to be made.

Simenovsky had popped in once or twice to check the progress being made.

'We're very pleased with your work so far,' he told Sandra, 'This could be one of our biggest catches to date.'

Sandra left at four o'clock. The drop was timed for eight. She wanted to rest for an hour before preparing herself.

The operation that night was in essence very simple. Mallette had been told one of the girls, Lucy, whom he was obviously attracted to, was having a birthday party, and could he come? In the past few weeks he had visited the club with Sandra about four times when all the girls, especially Lucy, would fuss over him.

Of course, he said, he would be delighted to attend. As it was a special occasion, Granny had bent the rules and allowed wine to be brought into the club.

Mallette's drink, of course, would be drugged. Not enough to stop him realizing what he was doing, but just the correct amount to make him lose his inhibitions as most people do at a certain level of alcohol intake or after some marijuana.

When Mallette was primed, Sandra and Lucy were to lead him into the bedroom and lie on the bed with him. Using their own instincts and talents they were to get him to make love to them, or at least indulge in heavy foreplay. Which would be filmed.

Sandra and Lucy had rehearsed the scene four times to make sure Mallette was in the correct position for the camera.

Their faces were not too prominent but they had to be clearly seen to be indulging in sex. They used one of the homosexual cameramen for the stand-in.

The operation seemed foolproof, but Granny and Sandra ran over it a dozen times, thinking out what could go wrong. Nothing, it appeared.

Sandra ran a deep bath when she arrived back at her flat. Stripping, she lay on her bed while the water cooled and let her body relax. She concentrated on the image of a white rose and soon her mind and body were completely at ease. This was a trick she had learnt while staying in one of the Notting Hill communes from a boy she shared a room with. It was the only advantage she gained from him, she claimed.

Twenty minutes later, feeling alert and sharp, she went for her bath. She had one foot in it when the phone rang.

'Hi there! How have you been? Long time no see and all that,' Viktor's voice said cheerily. It was double talk, letting Sandra know that what followed was to be taken as a straight message. 'I thought we might have coffee now.'

'I'm just going to have a bath. I'm going out tonight.'

'Oh, what a shame,' Viktor said. 'I'm just off to the country for a while. Are you sure you can't make it?'

Sandra sighed. By saying he was off to the country, he meant he had to see her immediately.

'Okay, darling,' she said. 'You know how to persuade a woman,' she chuckled. 'Where?'

'You know that over-priced coffee house beside the Londonderry Hotel? I'll be there in about ten minutes. 'Bye,' Viktor said and hung up.

Sandra slipped on a cat-suit over which she slung a fur coat. Viktor was waiting at a table beside a window.

'Hello, love,' she said, sitting down. 'How have you been? You're looking wonderful.'

'Oh, busy, busy,' he smiled. 'You know what it's like. You get caught up in this and that.'

The two coffees which Viktor had already ordered arrived. He leaned over towards Sandra and, still smiling, said seriously in a low tone, 'You're dropping the mark tonight, aren't you?'

'Yes,' Sandra replied, smiling back at him.

'Don't go.'

'What?' she said loudly.

'Quiet. Don't go. Don't be anywhere near the club tonight, Go to the theatre, the cinema, anywhere.'

'Have you gone mad? Do you know how long I've worked on this?'

Viktor nodded.

'I know. But I've had some news. It might not work out the way you think.'

'What are you talking about?' Sandra asked, looking worried.

'You don't have to know anything else. Follow my instructions and you'll be fine. Do you understand?'

Sandra nodded dumbly. She was totally confused.

'What about Granny? And Simenovsky? And Freddy?' she asked.

'Don't contact anyone,' he said urgently. 'I'll take care of it all.'

Sandra shook her head in bewilderment.

'But why?' she insisted. 'Why cancel it now?'

'You'll find out. And be thankful you followed your orders,' he said.

And when she did find out, she was not only thankful. She was terrified. For she realized what could have happened to her had she disobeyed Viktor's orders . . .

CHAPTER 6

I knew Hathaway Robbins for approximately forty-eight
hours. When I first met him I thought he was an intelligent,
self-confident, well-bred man of manners. A gentleman.
When I left him I saw him as a weak-willed, effete, pathetic
slob. It doesn't take long, you see, to find out a man's true
character. Especially after what I went through with Hath.

My first glimpse of him was through the rain-spattered
window of his dark blue Rolls-Royce. I was hitching back
from Glasgow having covered yet another demo. I was cold,
wet, and wondering what I was doing at the age of eighteen
standing by the side of the road with my thumb stuck out.
Not even the revolutionary fervour I had seen in Glasgow
was any consolation that day. I had been standing by the
side of the A74 for about half an hour when the Rolls pulled
up.

The window slid down and I peered in.

'Where are you headed?' the public school accent asked
me.

'London,' I shouted back.

'Hop aboard,' he smiled, taking a half-smoked cigar from
his mouth. 'I'm headed that way myself.'

Revolutionary I may have been, but I certainly wasn't
going to turn down the chance of a lift in comfort. I wouldn't
fawn all over him either, I decided, as I opened the thick
heavy door and slung my knapsack casually in the back as if
I was used to travelling in such style.

I climbed in, pushing myself into the corner, and stared
ahead. He drove off and didn't say anything for about ten
minutes. I kept sneaking glances at him. He looked in his
mid-thirties, and had fair, almost blond, wavy hair.

I was fascinated by his rounded face. It was so smooth,

as if he didn't have any pores. The car reeked of his after-shave. He was wearing a white open-neck shirt with a blue spotted cravat, blue trousers and white shoes. My ideal picture of a member of the Establishment.

His hands rested easily on the bottom of the steering wheel. They were of the same smoothness, pink as his face, and his nails, I remember, were highly buffed and perfectly shaped.

'Student?' he eventually asked, turning to me with a fixed smile.

'No.'

'Oh?'

I knew what that meant all right. He'd taken one look at the faded, patched jeans and my anorak covered with badges and immediately assumed I was studying.

'What do you do, then?' he asked.

'I'm a worker,' I muttered.

'*Really*? And who do you work for?'

'The cause,' I said priggishly.

'The *what*?' he laughed.

His laughter annoyed me. He seemed so smug.

'The cause,' I repeated. 'The cause of the people. The down-trodden classes who suffer because ninety per cent of the wealth in this country is owned by ten per cent of the population.'

'Like me, you mean,' he said pleasantly.

I didn't answer.

'So you're a Commie, then?' he went on.

Actually I never was, and never would be, a card-carrying member of the Party. But I didn't tell him that.

'And what's wrong with that?'

'Nothing, nothing,' he said. 'You don't have to get on the defensive. Only I agree with what someone once said about Communism – it's like prohibition. A good idea, but it just won't work.'

That did it! Sitting up, I pulled out a cheap cigarette, declining his offer of some fancy cigarettes, and began to argue with him. We argued all the way down to Manchester. By the time we reached the outskirts of the city, we were at least on first-name terms. Hathaway ('Call me "Hath" ')

85

infuriated me. Everything I said he had an answer for. And what's more, he'd actually read Marx and Lenin at University before going into the world of business and building his wealth up from nothing, through electronics factories.

The thing that really made me mad, of course, was that every time he answered one of my points I would scream and bang the walnut dashboard and jump up and down with frustration. Hath kept his cool the whole journey, never once raising his voice or becoming angry. *That's* what annoyed me.

It was dusk by the time we arrived in Manchester.

'Well,' he said. 'Thank you very much for joining me and making the time go by quickly.'

He was thanking *me*! After what I had called him, said to him and accused him of doing! I laughed. We lived in completely different worlds, our philosophies were galaxies apart, but not once had he talked down to me, I realized. I respected him for that. I was attracted by his intelligent discussion on an equal level with me. So while I thought it amusing he should be thanking me, at the same time I felt disappointment. Hitching through the dark is not my idea of fun.

He must have been reading my thoughts.

'Would you like something to eat before you go on your way?' he asked.

I hesitated. Taking a lift was one thing. But a meal? He might get ideas. And for all I knew he could have been a rapist. Although I doubted that, to be honest.

'I'd like the company,' he said. 'Think of it as milking the capitalists,' he laughed.

'Okay, I'll join you, thanks.'

'Good. We'll book in at the hotel first. Have you a change of clothes?' he asked, looking at my 'demo outfit'.

So that was it, I thought. I got the whole picture. Book into the hotel, dinner in the restaurant, and upstairs for a night-cap.

'Sorry, Hath,' I shook my head. 'It's no go. A meal, yes. But your hotel? I'm sorry, I'm not a pick-up.'

'Good Lord, I should think not!' he said, shocked. 'We're

86

not eating at the hotel. Anyway, I've booked a suite and if you're worried about changing, you can have the key while I wait in the lobby. Fair enough?'

I nodded.

'Where will you stay tonight?' he asked.

'I've got some friends in Manchester,' I said quickly. Which happened to be true. The only trouble was I had no idea where they lived. But if the worst came to the worst, I could find a cheap hotel and charge it up to *International Times* as part of expenses.

The hall porters looked down their noses at me when I strolled in with Hath, knapsack in hand. I handed it to one of them and said, 'Could you take this upstairs for me, *comrade*,' as a way of letting them know I was on their side, that I was working on their behalf. He turned his back and walked away!

But when Hath asked him, he quickly changed his tune and took it up to the suite. And these were some of the workers I was slogging up and down the country for!

Dinner was at the Slow Boat, where Hath was welcomed by the head waiter as if he was an old friend. I drank saki for the first time and the warm glow it gave me helped me relax. We had a five-course Chinese meal, which Hath insisted on ordering for me. There were all sorts of bits and pieces I'd never seen before. Sauces that made my mouth water just to look at them, meats so tender they literally melted in my mouth and wine that tasted like rose petals. What luxury! I loved every mouthful.

'So what do you think of capitalists now?' he grinned as I started into my lychees and syrup.

'Very funny,' I said. 'You haven't bought my loyalty for the price of a meal.'

'I'm glad to hear it,' he said raising his glass of 1964 Margaux, or something equally esoteric. 'To the revolution.'

I raised my glass, but couldn't drink. The look on Hath's face, the twinkle in his eyes as he laughed inwardly at the joke of us toasting the revolution in an exclusive restaurant, made me burst out laughing.

In the Rolls, he asked me where I wanted to go. I shrugged,

feeling warm and secure in the car, listening to music playing softly from the radio.

'How about a night-cap while you decide?'

'Perfect,' I said, wanting the night to go on forever, not having to think about my hitching back to London in the morning.

In his suite, he ordered a bottle of Krug champagne. We sat in huge leather armchairs at opposite ends of the room, our glasses in our hands, not saying anything.

'You know,' he finally said, 'despite your leftist nonsense, I like you. Cheers,' he added lifting his glass.

Whether it was the wine, the meal, the champagne, my feeling of warmth and contentment, or perhaps a combination of them all, I don't know. But suddenly Hath appeared as a handsome, kind, sexual man. I felt a slight tightening around my abdomen, and a longing which was centred between my thighs.

'Hath,' I said quietly. 'I want you. Now.'

He sat for a few seconds looking at me. The tension in my body was building up. My legs were beginning to move involuntarily as the ache between them increased. I closed my eyes. I did not hear him come across and stand over me. I opened my eyes and he took the glass out of my hand then pulled me up, kissing me fully on the mouth. My body was crying out for relief and I pressed tightly against him to ease the psychological, yet real, pain.

My breath was coming out in short gasps and I was making guttural, throaty sounds. I couldn't speak. He was hard. I felt him through my thin skirt, pushed against him, wanting him to enter me. Needing him to enter me.

'Slowly, my little one,' he whispered. 'Slowly.'

We fell to the floor, and I clawed at him, desperate to feel more of his body. But he took his time, would not be rushed by my crazy pleas. He slowly took my blouse and bra off me and knelt by my side, kissing my nipples, running his fingers over my stomach, lightly, delicately, driving me insane with desire. And then moving his hand down to my knee and running it lightly up the inside of my thigh, finally pressing his palm fully on my vulva. He kept his hand there, pushing down with his palm, his fingers stroking my already wet vagina. I couldn't believe the sensations. We were not yet naked and he had brought me to orgasm.

Tears were streaming down my cheeks, for the stabbing passion in my groin was now almost unbearable. I peeled my panties and skirt off, pleading with him to take me. I was hardly aware of him standing up and stripping, or sinking to his knees in front of me. I felt him lower himself on top of me, and kiss me passionately. His tongue pushed into my mouth just as he entered me.

Every nerve in my body responded. I was shaking as he slowly at first, and then faster, brought me to my second orgasm of the night, at the same time as he climaxed. We lay together on the floor for about ten minutes.

I turned to him, stroked his face, running my fingers round his mouth and thanked him.

He said nothing. He had been silent all through our love-making.

I stood up and automatically went through to the bedroom where I lay on the bed, a smile of deep satisfaction on my face. Hath had done in one night what twenty or more others had found impossible in over a year. He had made me experience not one, but two, incredible orgasms in one night!

The thought flicked across my mind that perhaps well-bred gentlemen were better bed-partners than their lower-class equals. Making a woman feel feminine, giving her satisfaction is not something which comes instinctively. I realized. It's learnt along with all the other trappings of culture.

The realization shocked and excited me at the same time. From my early days in the Gorbals, through the insane scenes I'd been in, my total dissatisfaction with sex until that night, I'd always had the feeling that there was some-thing better. I thought I would have found it by trying to create an alternative society. But, honestly, were nights like the one I spent with Hath not what I was aiming for?

I remember these thoughts so clearly now. I was genuinely confused, only certain of one thing. I'd had two orgasms that night. And I was very, very happy.

The next morning Hath wanted to make love again, but I'm always sleepy in the morning, so he didn't insist.

We drove to London. Hath suggested dinner that night and I agreed. I felt somewhat hypocritical during the day as I typed out my copy about the Scottish demo scene for *IT*, thinking all the while about meeting Hath later on. I'd asked him to take me to Trader Vic's, never having been there, but I had heard it was expensive.

Hath had called it a 'tourist trap' but agreed to meet me in the lobby of the Hilton at eight. I borrowed a simple black cocktail dress from my flat-mate, having no decent clothes of my own, something I had never really noticed before.

What a meal! I was thrilled just by the size of the menu alone! I had some of those funny rum cocktail things, spare ribs and sweet and sour prawns with crackers, Gambler's Duck and about six side dishes with all sorts of meat and vegetables in them. I asked for some saki, and finished up with a Calypso coffee, made of coffee, Tia Maria and cream.

Not even in my wildest dreams had I imagined food like that existing!

Hath kept laughing at me through the meal.

'I don't know how you can eat that tourist slop,' he said.

But to me it was heaven. I relished every mouthful. Not a scrap was left. As they say in those romantic stories in women's magazines, I felt as if I was floating. So when Hath suggested his place, I nodded. I was ready for anything!

His 'place' turned out to be a small *pied-à-terre* in Cadogan Place, Belgravia. His real home, as I was to find out later, was in Surrey, a mansion where he kept his wife, three children, and a pony. But that was later, after I had discovered a little more about the habits of well-bred gentlemen.

'Let's have a bath,' Hath said as soon as we were in the door.

'A bath?' I said, thinking he had gone crazy.

He showed me the bathroom. Most of it was taken up by a round, sunken green bath. Everything else was onyx and gold. The water gurgled out from two gold taps shaped like fish and Hath added some bubble foam. We stripped quickly

nd laughing and splashing like two children we made love
the water.

That, as I soon discovered, was only the *hors d'oeuvres*. He
d me through to the bedroom where – and I couldn't
elieve my eyes – he had a four-poster bed, which looked as
g as a squash court to me!

Our love-making was even better than in Manchester.
ath brought me to orgasm by oral sex alone, not letting me
ove until I had been satisfied. Being more sober, also, I had
chance to get a good look at Hath. He was equipped with
e sort of manhood every girl dreams about.

We were awake most of the night, and it was only *my*
xhaustion which forced us to finish. I snuggled down close
Hath feeling the silk sheets rub deliciously against my
red body. This is more like it, I thought, as I fell asleep.
his is where I belong. And I didn't give a hoot if anyone
lled me a snob.

Hath jumped out of bed at 7.30 am, kissed me lightly
n the cheek, showered, dressed in a pin-stripe suit and
ft for the office. I stretched out in the bed, enjoying the
armth, my body completely relaxed. I was just drifting
ff to sleep when a maid appeared at the door carrying a
ay loaded with bacon, eggs, mushrooms, marmalades, a
lver tea pot and a china cup and saucer.

I ate slowly, feeling hungry. I chewed each mouthful
owly, enjoying the rich tastes. The sun was shining
rough the window and I loved the feeling of spoilt luxury. A
it different from my normal breakfast of coffee and toast!

But it was that thought which brought the first pang of
uilt. *What was I doing?* Lying in an antique bed which
ust have cost thousands; feeling silk sheets against me;
ating a breakfast as big as my normal dinner and surrounded
y lavish wealth. And two-thirds of the people of the world
ere starving in hovels.

I felt sick. Really sick. I began crying, disgusted at myself,
anting to wipe out the past two days. I knew that was
npossible, which only made it worse. I had betrayed my
eliefs, my friends, *myself*. I was miserable. I did not feel I

wanted to die. I wanted more – not to have existed at all.

Why me? I kept asking myself. Why me? Because I had responded to Hath's sexual advances? But I had wanted to make love as much as him. He had even called me a good lover.

And then I stopped crying. Of course, I realized, Hath was attracted to *me*. Why else would he spend so much time and money on me. A man in his position could afford to buy his women. I had not betrayed my friends. *I had found a way to break into the Establishment we all hated.* What was to stop me spying on the ruling classes, and passing the knowledge to my revolutionary friends?

The answer, quite simply, struck me as I lay in Hath's bed. Everything would stop me. Because I had no idea what to do.

But the idea was there, and I knew something would turn up sooner or later. It was sooner.

I dressed quickly, wanting to see Alec and discuss my new tactics with him. He would know what to do if anyone did. It was while I was brushing my hair that I noticed the envelope stuck in the corner of the mirror, with my name scrawled across it.

Inside was a ten-pound note and a letter. It was a simple message. It was to change my life.

> 'Thanks', it said. 'It was wonderful. See
> you around sometime. Love Hath.'

At first I was calm, not believing – no, not wanting to believe – what I had read. And then anger set in. I felt cheap, used and dirty. I looked around Hath's neat flat. I wanted to smash it, rip his precious silk sheets, destroy his antique furniture. But he'd probably laugh and buy some more.

I sat down and lit a cigarette, letting the ash fall on the floor. It was while I was looking at it on top of his carpet that my anger was replaced by a determination to make him feel what he was – a chauvinist pig, the sort Marx must have had in mind when he wrote about women being seen by the bourgeoisie as prostitutes.

In the kitchen I found a note from the maid to Hath saying she would be back in a few days and to phone if he needed anything. Perfect. I had the place to myself. It was ten o'clock so I had plenty of time.

I left the house, but not before fastening the safety catch to make sure the door would not lock. Using some of the ten pounds I caught a cab back to my flat. Grabbing a basket, I filled it with all the dirty washing I could find – my own and my flat mate's, I found a length of rope in the kitchen and took another cab back to Belgravia.

In the flat, I hung the rope across the front room, dipped a couple of dresses, some pants and bras in soapy water and hung them up on the line. I scattered the rest of the clothes round the room.

I chain-smoked, and as each ashtray filled, I tipped it on the floor. I made myself some cheese sandwiches and after half-eating them, crumbled them over the kitchen floor, as well as leaving bits of crust and cheese over the bed.

By four o'clock Hath's love-nest looked like a drunken gypsy's kitchen.

I rushed out and bought some cakes and prepared a pot of tea. Not knowing exactly what time Hath would be back, I poured myself a large gin and tonic and settled down in the armchair, over which I had spread a pair of damp denims.

At exactly 5.30 pm I heard the outside door open and Hath whistling his way along the narrow hall. He froze when he came into the front room.

'What the hell is going on here?' he roared, his face red with anger.

I smiled sweetly at him.

'Hello, darling. Did you have a nice day?' I asked before waving my hand round the room. 'Oh, this? I've moved in. You don't mind, do you? We can make love every night now.'

'Like hell! You're getting out right now!' he yelled, as he started to gather up the dirty clothes. 'And I mean *now*!'

I looked at him, pretending to be confused.

'But Hath, darling, I've worked it al. out. You can have half the wardrobe . . .'

'Out! Out!' he screamed, dropping the clothes and walking over to me, his fists clenched.

To be honest, I was frightened, but tried not to show it.

'But Hath, where can I go? Ten pounds is hardly enough for anything nowadays. Even for a girl like me.'

'You can have twenty pounds! Just get out.'

'Why don't we talk this through like sensible people, Hath?'

He stood staring at me for a few seconds. I thought he was going to hit me. I held my breath. But he turned slowly and sank into a chair.

'That's better,' I said, relieved. 'Would you like some tea?' I asked, pulling a cloth away from a tray piled with the cakes I'd bought, a silver teapot and two cups. I poured the tea, which luckily was still warm.

'If you're not out of here with your rubbish in ten minutes, I'm calling the police,' he said, ignoring my offer of tea.

'Oh, I don't think you'd do that, Hath,' I said, not looking at him as I chose a cake. Then I turned to him, looking him straight in the eyes. 'Do you know how old I am, darling?'

His eyes bulged and his mouth fell open.

'Oh, my God! Oh, no!' He ran his hands through his hair, hunching forward on the chair.

'Right, Hath,' my anger returning. 'Three months off sixteen. I'm told the police don't take too kindly to dirty old men tampering with *children*.'

'Oh, God, what have I done?' he moaned pathetically. 'I'm an important man. This could ruin me. The scandal would finish me.' And then he told me about his wife and children.

As he did I fought the temptation to smash the teapot across his complacent face. But I knew that would get me nowhere.

'What do you want?' he finally asked me, looking frightened. 'Tell me, for God's sake.'

I said nothing for a few minutes, enjoying his fear.

'Not much,' I said quietly. 'Just enough to give me a start. The sort of start you'd give your own daughter. I've got ambitions, ideas. I'm not waiting for every Tom, Dick or Harry to come along and take me to bed for the price of a meal. I want a respectable job, nice clothes, a flat and decent boy-friends. I'm still very young,' I pointed out, reminding

...im of what he thought he had done.

'How much do you want?' he asked, in a weak voice.

'A thousand pounds.'

'Impossible,' he shook his head. 'I don't keep that sort of money in the flat.'

'How much *have* you here?'

'Four hundred pounds.'

'Sorry, I don't come that cheap. Or go. I'll stay the night and tomorrow we can collect the money.'

He stood up and walked over to a painting. Taking it down, he fiddled with the combination lock of a wall safe and pulled out some money. He counted it.

'This is all I've got in the flat. I want you out now. There's eight hundred pounds here.'

I nodded.

'I'm not greedy. That'll do,' I said, holding my hand out.

'Now go!'

'As soon as I've got my clothes together,' I smiled, collecting my bits and pieces.

He stood silently watching me. When I had gathered everything, I told him I was leaving. He didn't answer.

I put on my coat, asking him to hold my basket. He refused. I walked to the front door, and he stared at me from the lounge, hatred written all over his face.

I opened the door, but turned back, one hand still on the handle, and looked him in the eyes.

'You pharasaic son-of-a-bitch! This is *not* the last you'll hear from me. You'd better sweat, baby!'

Laughing, I slammed the door behind me and ran into the street looking for a taxi.

My laughter did not last long. What Hath had done to me could not be wiped out by petty blackmail. In sexual terms, I had experienced the finest two nights of my life. Now I knew there was nothing wrong with me. What a wonderful feeling that was. To know I could enjoy sex; could find men who would satisfy me. As far as I was concerned, you see, I had made love properly for the first time. He had opened my eyes to sex. I felt like a *woman*. And the feeling *was* wonderful.

But in terms of the class war, I experienced what I had known in theory over the years. A bourgeois attitude bred the type of men who treated women like fancy cars. To be looked at, enjoyed and then put away until the next time they wanted to use them. And I saw Hath as only representative of his class.

The hurt and pain he had given me was to be with me for a long time. Everything I did in the future, I swore then, would be only to hit back at people like Hath. The powerful, the influential, the wealthy. The Establishment.

Not even the horrific times that were to follow affected me as much as Hath's simple ten-word note that morning.

CHAPTER 7

Sandra sat in the Bayswater safe-house watching Viktor thumb through some sheets of paper.

'Is that Czechoslovakian?' she asked, glancing at what looked like hieroglyphics to her.

'No, no, Russian,' Viktor muttered, looking up. 'I speak Russian as fluently as English.'

Sandra was impressed. His English was word perfect.

They had been in the safe-house for half an hour. She had gone to the cinema the night before, as instructed, and was now waiting for Viktor to explain the sudden change of plans. He was in no hurry to do so, and kept muttering to himself in Russian or Czech as he pored over the documents which had come to him via the diplomatic pouch.

Finally, he put the papers in a brief-case and turned to Sandra, smiling.

'And how are you, Sandra?' he asked.

'I'm fine, Viktor,' she said, amazed. 'Please, what is going on?'

Viktor stood up and walked to the window. Outside it was raining and cars could be heard splashing their way along the road.

'The club's closed,' he said, still watching the street.

'Closed? Why? What happened?' Sandra poured the questions out.

'And Granny and Simenovsky are at this moment on their way back to Prague to face a disciplinary committee,' he added, ignoring her queries.

Sandra felt weak. What was coming?

'I'm afraid last night was a disaster as far as the drop was concerned,' he went on. 'You see, our whole operation was almost blown sky-high, as I think you say in this country.'

He paused and lit a cigarette.

'Viktor, *please* tell me what happened!' she demanded.

He came across and sat opposite her in one of the large armchairs, settling back.

'It's very simple, really,' he began. 'Last night everyone turned up as arranged – except you. As you know, it was strictly invitation-only, for obvious reasons. But two uninvited men arrived, and asked to be allowed in. They caused a bit of a scene at the door, so Granny came to explain the situation to them. They refused to leave, saying they were personal friends of Freddy Mallette, who had not yet arrived, and he had asked them along,' Viktor sighed as if bored and disappointed.

Sandra was perched on the edge of the couch, her face serious.

'Eventually Simenovsky came out and explained yet again it was an invitation-only party. It was only when Mallette arrived and said yes, he did know the men, and he had invited them, that Granny and Simenovsky let the men in. So we had two outsiders taking part in a carefully rehearsed operation. But that could have been handled had it not been for one fact. They were DI6 agents. Luckily my brother Mikhail, who you remember is the head of the London station, popped in for a few minutes and recognized them. He was furious, as you will appreciate,' Viktor chuckled. 'He went straight to the Embassy and called the club, cancelling the operation and telling them to have a normal party. And ordering Simenovsky and Granny to report to him later.'

'So will the operation take place another time?'

'Impossible, my love, impossible,' Viktor said. 'We always suspected DI6 were watching the club. Now they'll be tailing Mallette and as soon as we approach him they'll be on to us.'

'But why close the club?' she asked, perplexed. 'Not that I'm sorry. I always thought it was a dingy hole. And why have Granny and Simenovsky been pulled back to the Centre?'

'The club had outlasted its usefulness,' he replied. 'And Granny and Simenovsky broke every rule in the book letting two strangers in on a drop night. They jeopardized our whole network in this country which has taken years to build up. They won't be seen in London again,' he added, a strange smile playing round his lips.

Sandra stared at him. There was something wrong with the story, something she could not identify immediately. Then she saw it.

'But why did Freddy say it was all right for the men to go in? He knew it was a closed party. I'd told him not to invite anyone, and he swore he wouldn't. I mean, he didn't want other people knowing about his little foibles.'

Viktor smiled that strange, twisted smile again.

'Exactly,' he said flatly. 'Freddy was told to allow them in. But Granny and Simenovsky should have resisted,' he added quickly. 'We knew they would not, however. We . . .'

'Freddy was *told*! By who?' Sandra interrupted.

'By my brother, who had recruited him about two years ago.'

Sandra gasped.

'You mean . . . you mean . . . the whole thing was a set-up?'

Viktor nodded.

'Why, for Heaven's sake?' Sandra's eyes flickered angrily.

'Two reasons, although one doesn't really concern you,' Viktor said. 'Firstly, it was your first real practical test, in which you did very well. Secondly, to get rid of Simenovsky and Granny, who still had too much of the old school methods about them. The other thing which happened last night, which I didn't tell you, was that the club was raided by Special Branch, who took away our special equipment.'

Sandra was so staggered she could not think clearly.

'Who . . . who told DI6?' she stammered.

'We did,'

'What?' It was becoming lunatic now.

'No, it's not how it sounds. The men are double agents. The whole thing was engineered for them to "stumble" on the operation. Right now they're probably being congratulated and being given a pay rise, which if the structure's still the same as it was a few years ago, they will badly need.'

Sandra's mind was whirling.

'And Freddy? He's with *us*?'

'Yes, but until last night only my brother and I knew that. The Special Branch, of course, now think they've saved Freddy from a fate worse than death. Which is perfect. We'll be able to use him again in a little while.' Viktor stretched his arms. 'And now you see why you could not turn up at the club,' he grinned.

Sandra reached for her handbag and found her cigarettes. Lighting one, she thought that whoever called espionage a world of dirty tricks certainly coined the right phrase. And a further thought, one which made her tense her body at the realization. If the STB could do this to Simenovsky and Granny because they were dissatisfied, they would surely do the same to her if anything went wrong. She looked across at Viktor.

He was gazing at her, smiling pleasantly. Knowing exactly what was running through her mind . . .

'So you were not impressed with our little club?' Mikhail Pavlenko asked Sandra in a St John's Wood safe-house.

Mikhail, like his brother, was tall and fair-haired. He looked about ten years older than Viktor, and more relaxed in his approach. His angular face was lightly tanned, and he had piercing blue eyes which never seemed to smile, even when he was laughing. But again, like his brother, Mikhail seemed to like Sandra and although it was their first meeting, she was completely at ease.

'No, I didn't,' she answered. 'It was neither one thing or another. And the atmosphere was as cold as a fish shop.'

Mikhail laughed.

'You do know, of course, who designed it?' he asked.

Sandra nodded.

'You, darling,' she smiled. 'You may be the best station officer in the world, but when it comes to night-clubs I'm sorry, but you have a lot to learn. I mean,' she added, leaning forward in the modern easy chair she was sitting on, 'where were the back-up facilities to bring the marks in? I didn't hear of any.'

'We do have a catalogue, you know,' Mikhail protested.

'We're not altogether amateur at this game.'

'The catalogue!' Sandra laughed sarcastically. 'It's fragmented, has no link-up system. The whole underworld is connected in some way or another,' Sandra told him. 'Your catalogue hardly scrapes the surface!'

Mikhail had stopped smiling and listened intently.

'Go on,' he muttered. 'Go on.'

'With only one or two shops and a club, the chances are low that a big fish will wander in. It's laughable,' she said, warming up to a subject in which she knew she was expert. 'It's fine with someone like Freddy Mallette who was in the picture from the start. And Viktor tells me you've got a couple of call-girls working for you, ready to blackmail if and when they get the chance. Well, Mikhail, it doesn't work that way in the world I've been living in, honey.' She paused, waiting to see Mikhail's reaction. There was none. His eyes were still, and he seemed to be looking through Sandra.

'No prostitute worth anything would try obvious blackmail. She'd lose the mark forever. And the word would soon spread.'

She sat back, resting her head on the chair, pushing her breasts out. Mikhail's eyes moved over her.

'All you say is true, of course,' he said. 'There is a huge, grey world we know very little about. That's why I wanted to see you today. We have changed our basic operation in which you were to be involved. Instead . . .'

'What was it?' Sandra asked.

Mikhail shook his head.

'It doesn't concern you now. Suffice to say it was smaller than the operation we presently have in mind.'

He stood up and walked across to an old-fashioned mantelpiece and leant on it. A motorbike roared by noisily outside.

'We want you, using your specialist knowledge of the *demi-monde*, to set up a network along the lines you have just indicated,' he said. 'And money, by the way, will be no object.'

So this was it! At last, she thought. There was no point in asking Mikhail what the object of creating a net was. He would not tell her. But it would not be difficult to work out.

'The personal arrangement for you is satisfactory?' he asked, breaking into her thoughts.

'Yes, thank you,' she nodded. 'When do I start?'

'As soon as you're ready,' Mikhail said. 'But there's no rush. You have a proverb, I think, which says "Slowly, slowly, catch a monkey." That's exactly what we're going to do.'

The STB had made an ideal choice with Sandra. Not only did she understand the sometimes confusing connections within the underworld, she knew many girls in the 'profession', or 'working girls' as they preferred to be called. She knew which ones to trust and who was in the pay of organized crime syndicates. The latter made up more than most people, including Mikhail and his bosses, realized. For although it may look as if prostitution in London (and in any big city, in fact) is a collection of individual girls, sometimes protected by a pimp, Sandra knew from bitter experience that most girls are controlled by three or four vice rings, in deadly competition with each other. Sandra also knew that to interfere with this organized crime could lead to her flat being burnt and herself being beaten up and even killed. She had known girls who had become involved with the rackets, tried to get out, and were never heard of again.

She had been lucky. She had been caught up with Maltese gangsters years before. And managed to escape. But the lessons she had learnt made her wary.

She dealt mainly with Mikhail during the setting-up of the net. And while he had said money was limitless, everything had to be accounted for. Sandra had to answer for everything she spent, or advised them to buy.

She had decided at the start not to set up another club immediately. 'That would be falling into the same trap as before,' she explained to Mikhail. 'And a total waste of money.' Mikhail was doubly impressed.

'We set up a massage parlour first,' she suggested. 'There are nearly fifty already within the square mile of Soho,' she went on. 'So we're up against some competition. Some of them, like the one in Pall Mall, do actually give a straight service. But that's not quite our scene, darling!' she laughed.

Location was vital. Finally they decided on a basement store in Piccadilly, near the Services Club, opposite Green Park.

'That's near enough Soho for word to get round,' she reasoned. 'But far enough away not to be connected with the mass of porn merchants that hang out there.'

It had taken a month and a lot of leg work by Sandra to find the parlour. She had given up seeing most of her clients, but the STB's financial arrangement did not leave her short of money.

Furnishing, or fitting the parlour out for espionage purposes, was far easier. Sandra herself designed the lay-out along with an architect provided by Mikhail. Clients, or 'yobs' as Mikhail called targets, entered a small reception area which was oak-panelled and had a few oil paintings hanging on the walls. A deep red, thick carpet with an oriental circular rug covered the floor. A smartly dressed girl sat behind a bow desk, an appointments pad in front of her. If the client had to wait, there was an electric coffee percolator and a tray of biscuits on a small table beside the desk, for him to have if he wanted them. Six leather easy chairs were lined up against the wall opposite the desk. It was Mikhail's idea to put a framed scroll on the wall behind the desk, showing the club was a member of some fictitious Masseurs' Association.

To the left of the receptionist, two thick red velvet curtains hung on a bamboo pole. These hid the entrance to the parlour itself. Through them, the client would walk down a narrow corridor passing leather-studded doors on his right. He would reach the bathing area at the end of the corridor, on his left, where he would have a shower, being supplied with a small towel by his masseuse and given the number of the cubicle he was to come to after his shower. There were four showers, enough for normal use. Outside the shower area a long brown leather bench was placed under a solarium.

The price of a massage was high, but not so high a civil servant could not afford it. The whole emphasis of the place was dignified. Classical music was piped around the whole parlour.

Inside the cubicles, more brown leather benches were placed under spotlights. A trolley with creams and bottles of cologne stood near the door. In every cubicle a large, thick cardboard poster showing a muscular diagram of the human body took up most of one wall opposite the door and beside the bench. It was a varnished poster. Deliberately. One of the pupils in the drawing's eyes was a camera lens. For the whole parlour had been divided neatly by a sound-proofed wall. Behind the wall, cameras were trained into each cubicle. The peeping area was approximately one-third of the cubicles. Enough room for the two technicians always present. The entrance to the 'back-room', as it was nicknamed was at the end of the corridor, opposite the shower rooms. A large picture of a tennis star could be removed to reveal a panel in the wall with a small hole in it. When a security bolt-key was inserted, the panel swung open.

There were four girls who did the actual work. A Chinese girl, a Swedish girl and two London girls. All were personally known to Sandra. All of them trusted her and she paid them highly. None of them knew, or even suspected, that the back-room existed.

Sandra and Mikhail argued over the installation of the microphones and monitors. Mikhail wanted two television monitors in each room. Sandra said that was unnecessary as her girls always provided the 'extras' for the client while he was on the couch, and if two monitors were put in, the whole cubicle would have to be reorganized. Which meant the whole parlour being redesigned to have the back-room repositioned. Sandra won. Two loudspeakers, for the stereo-phonic piped music, were put in the corners of the cubicle, facing the bench. Each had a switch on a small panel inserted above the lower edge of the speaker. Beside the switch was a clear plastic dome, which glowed when the sound system was on. One of the domes was a television camera lens used for monitoring only.

The microphones were slotted into the track rod used for the spotlights, each bug being insulated in soft foam and placed in a small plastic box to look like a capacitor normally used by electricians.

Sandra employed a Public Relations Consultancy to help build up an image for the club. And the last thing she did was to choose a name. It was simple and effective. She called it 'The Exclusive Massage Parlour'.

Finally, the parlour was ready to go into business. All it needed was a dry run to test the furnishings. Lord Freddy Mallette was the man chosen for the test. He was delighted, of course. He showered, and came trotting out holding his towel in front of him, grinning sheepishly. He chose the Chinese girl and they disappeared into the cubicle.

In the back-room, Sandra and Mikhail watched on the monitor as Freddy lay on the bench, the towel still in front of him. He pulled it away when the girl started to massage his legs.

Sandra giggled.

'What a shame the drop didn't go through at the club,' she said. 'I never knew he could offer such a prize!'

The cameraman shot his frames rapidly, using a large soundproofed motor wind. The camera, a Nikon, was loaded with a special 72-frame film.

Freddy waved the girl away when she asked him to turn over. He asked her what she charged for 'extras'.

'What *do* you mean?' she asked, pretending to look shocked.

'I want a complete relaxation massage,' he said. 'To ease my tense muscles,' he added, looking pointedly at his erection. 'And I want the best,' he demanded.

'I'm afraid that's an extra ten pounds,' she said. 'And you give it to me.'

Sandra nodded. She had told the girls they could keep all the money they earned from 'relief massage' as it was called.

The girl, a petite little thing with long black shiny hair, flung her head back. With both hands she held her hair at the back of her neck and leaned forward from the waist. She ran her tongue down the length of his penis and back again. She lightly flicked her tongue over the top, before putting her lips round it, and slowly took him into her mouth.

She moved her head back and forwards for a few minutes

when Freddy suddenly grasped the side of the bench and gasped. The girl straightened and, smiling at him, moved over to the trolley, and with her back to him pulled out a tissue and wiped her mouth.

The cameraman sat back, his job done. Sandra was smiling at the success of the furnishings. Mikhail was nodding. And when the film was developed, they were perfect. Freddy's comment on seeing them was, 'God, I *am* getting fat. I'd better have some more of those massages to tone me up.'

The massage parlour was, in every way, a success. The first strands of the net had been woven. But, Sandra realized, it was only the beginning. The net would have to widen. For she was becoming aware they were after some very big fish indeed . . .

CHAPTER 8

*andra broke down several times during the following account
*f her experiences. The recording was made in a flat in St John's
*Vood, because she felt her own house was being watched. I never
*ound out if this was true. As with other transcripts, I have
dited it.

ARR

Vith the money Hath had given me, I rented a flat in
*rebeck Street, off Shepherd's Market, Mayfair. It was
*mall, neat, completely self-contained and in a smart block.
* was thrilled! Living in Mayfair, money in the bank, and
* new direction to my life. Wasn't *I* going to be the one who
*vould hit at the soft underbelly of capitalism? Oh, yes, I
*rmly believed I was going to be a one-woman fifth column
*vorking on behalf of the revolutionaries and workers.

But as my money dwindled, and I pounded the streets
*or two weeks from one employment agency to another
*etting nothing I thought suitable for my new cause, my
*eartfelt resolutions began to crumble. It was all very well
*edicating my life to all-out sexual class warfare, and a
*vonderful feeling having a burning passion to destroy the
*ystem. The trouble was, where did I start the fire?

The next two years turned out to be hell. I don't want to
*alk about them in too much detail, as I can still feel the
*ain and degradation I went through. And I know it's been
*aid before, and it will be again. But if any young girl is
*hinking of coming to London and selling her body to make
*ome quick money, my advice is forget it. As you'll see I was
*acky. Very lucky. I managed to get out.

I was finally offered a job as an assistant to a sales con-
*erence organizer. Basically, I had to find suitable hotels for

the conferences and arrange all entertainment for the evenings. This could be anything from a night at the National Opera House to a visit to Paul Raymond's Revuebar for nude shows. As well as providing women for expense account intercourse.

This was easier than I thought. I was introduced to a Roy Brewer-Jones, the PR for the Royal Club, a smart gambling club in Curzon Street. I couldn't stand him. He was what would be called in Scotland a 'right wee nyaff' – i.e. a creep. He claimed to have been an actor at one time until illness forced him off the stage. When I met him, he had not long joined the Royal Club, and as far as I was concerned was nothing more than a smooth-operating pimp.

This is how it would work. Brewer-Jones would keep in touch with people like my boss, and know when businessmen were coming into town. It was up to me to introduce the Chairman or Secretary of the group to him, when Brewer-Jones would invite about half a dozen of them to the Royal for a free meal, and hint at a free membership.

They would go to the club, have a meal, lose a few hundred or thousand pounds on the tables, and everyone was happy. Brewer-Jones always gave me a small percentage of the takings, which kept me happy. If the men wanted women, then Brewer-Jones was only too willing to pull out his little black book (I'm not joking about that – it really was a little black book. I tell you, that man was every cliché you could think of!) with a list of girls in London who seemed to sit at the end of a phone waiting to be asked out by businessmen from Bradford, Leeds and other provincial paradises.

And, as I was learning fast, it's always better to hide your feelings about someone if they can be of use to you. Brewer-Jones not only showed me the connection between prostitution and the straight world, he introduced me into gambling circles, where I soon became recognized and accepted. And more important, I began to build up my own list of girls – which was to come in very handy later on.

I went to bed with a few of the businessmen myself, and took the money they insisted on giving me. I reckon the money – which ranged from £25 to £200 on one occasion –

helped salve their petty consciences.

They were buying a woman, which is different from going and having an affair. If their wives ever found out, they could use the old line, 'Well, love, there comes a time in every man's life when he wonders what it would be like with someone else and I only bought her after all and can't even remember her name and of course it was terrible.' So I took their money, and often used some of it to help some of the girls who were in trouble with police fines or medical bills.

I was, don't forget, at the forefront of the New Revolution! Using the capitalists to help the tools of the bourgeoisie, as I saw the girls, was my little attempt at doing something positive.

But then I became stupid. I had this crazy idea of opening a bank account to fund the work of my revolutionary friends. The notion came to me one night while I was lying in bed with a Scottish businessman called John Wilson. I was bored, as he had insisted on performing only oral sex on me – for an hour non-stop! It was a wonder he could speak!

His wallet was lying on the bedside cabinet on my side and he asked me to pass it to him – for my payment, I presume. As I did so, some photographs fell out. Nice family shots with Mum, Dad and the kids.

'Wife and children?' I smiled.

'Well . . . um . . . yes, in fact,' he spluttered.

'I wonder what she'd say if she knew what you'd been doing tonight?' I joked.

He didn't think it funny. 'You wouldn't would you?' he said, sitting upright looking terrified.

'Wouldn't what?' I teased.

'Tell her.' He still thought I was serious.

'Oh, I don't know, sweetheart,' I cooed, 'I think I'll drop her a line and let her know how good you were in bed. Especially at *you-know-what* . . .' I was toying with a business card he'd given me earlier on at the Royal. (These men really open themselves to all sorts of trouble. A couple of bottles of champagne and they'd show you their birth certificates if they carried them. I've seen it thousands of times in clubs. It's a shame they're not worth it!)

Anyway, Wilson jumped out of bed, dressed quickly and emptied his wallet on the bed. There was £150 in it. He pushed it at me.

'That's all I've got. Do you promise not to say anything if I give it to you?'

It was pathetic! The grovelling little hypocrite!

'That'll be fine,' I said, coolly. 'For now.'

I used the money to open my 'Fighting Fund'. I tried it once more and was given a hundred pounds. But that was the end. Word got back to my boss. He was flaming! Neither of the companies would ever book through him again, he said, because of what I'd done. I was fired on the spot. Which is the real reason why no call-girl who seriously wants to make money will try blackmail at that level. She'll lose everything. Like I almost did.

I drifted for a while. Brewer-Jones didn't want to know me after what I'd done. But a few of the girls, feeling sorry for me, put some men my way, whom I would 'entertain' for the evening. My money was running low, and I was becoming depressed. One of the girls suggested I became a hostess at the Canary Club, off Oxford Street, which she'd heard was discreet and full of VIPs and top brass. Facing the prospect of losing my flat, I went along and was given a job.

The club was tied in with an escort agency at Marble Arch, the idea being that the John would pick us up there, take us for a meal, and then we'd steer him to the club. If he wanted to take us to bed later, either at his hotel or my place, then he would have to buy two bottles of champagne at least, at £25 a bottle, which was how the club made its money. The girls kept the 'presents' the Johns gave them.

I don't know where the girl who told me about the club got the idea it was exclusive, but the Johns I met were even bigger slobs than the salesmen I'd known.

(Sandra kept a diary of her experiences at the agency, for reasons she was not quite sure of then. But later said it was in case she did come across a VIP and she'd have accurate details of his likes and dislikes. The following are verbatim extracts from the diary.
ARR)

Naren – Indian

A shy, quiet man who only came to the agency because he said he didn't know how to chat up girls. Said he'd had this dream all his life of being able to attract women, but it was only a dream. Very frustrated and wondered if he'd done the right thing in taking me out. Took me to an Indian restaurant in Albemarle Street. Held my hand most of the night, making it difficult for me to eat my meal. Liked my dress because it wasn't too flashy. Obviously a lonely man. Didn't know how to approach subject of sex and when I brought it up at the Canary said he didn't like my forwardness, paid for two bottles of champagne and left.

Hussein – Arab

Well-dressed, young and pushy. I asked him why he came to the agency. Told me he didn't want the hassle of talking to girls in discos. He liked sex and just wanted a good fuck, he said. Didn't want a meal, so took him straight to the club. Bought two bottles of champagne, taking one away with us. Went back to his place, a flat off Park Street. I did most of the talking. Wanted anal intercourse and I let him have it. He thumped away at me like a steam-hammer and then complained he was tired but not yet satisfied. We fucked again, this time straight and more slowly. Said I was 'amazing' and could he see me again. Paid well (£100.00) and wanted intercourse again. I was too tired and left.

Shaun – Irish businessman

Small, heavily built, and very strong. Wanted a dominant lady, he said. I told him I didn't go in for that sort of thing. He was very disappointed. Took me to Churchill's and then on to the Val Bonne, which he said was 'too young' for him. I suggested the Canary, and we went back there. He saw another girl he liked, and asked if I would take part in a threesome. I shrugged and Paula joined us. Had plenty of cash and bought six bottles of champagne. Took us back to the Dorchester. Asked us to play with each other while he watched. I hadn't done this before and didn't want to do it, but Paula knew the ropes and did most of the work. He masturbated. Wanted us to suck him off and told us what to do. I took his penis and Paula licked his balls. It was difficult,

but good fun. Gave us £100 each, and told us to suck hi
toes while he masturbated! We said no, and left. He wa
marked down at the agency as a good bet.

(*Sandra's diary has about fifty entries like the above, bu
claims these three are typical of the types that visit escor
agencies. Later, when she ran one herself, she kept more detaile
files on her clients.* ARR

I was making money, being taken out for meals, buyin
nice clothes and was actually saving. But I felt miserable
Empty. I was being used by men. Doing nothing to put m
theories of helping the underprivileged into action. But I wa
young yet, I told myself, coming up for my twenty-first birth
day. Plenty of time left once I had enough money for . .
And that's it! I didn't know what for. As things turned out,
was lucky to have *any* time left. In fact, I was lucky to se
my twenty-second birthday, but I'll explain.

I was hostessing in the club one night not long after m
twenty-first birthday. The place was practically empty as i
was not yet 10.30 pm. A few of us sat round a table sipping
coffee or Coke, waiting for the Johns to appear. The manager
a Maltese called Michael, walked over to us.

'Sandra, can you come into my office now?' he asked.

In his office, the most luxurious part of the club I thought
a thick-set, dark-skinned man sat behind the desk. He wa
wearing a camel coat slung over his shoulders, and a two
piece dark-blue mohair suit with a blue silk shirt and whit
tie. In the corner another man leaned against the wall. He
too, was dark-skinned and had a long, evil-looking face. Hi
hands were in the pockets of his dark coat and he scowle
at me.

'This is Mr Stavros,' Michael said, waving his hand a
the man behind the desk. 'He owns the Canary Club.'

I nodded politely, wondering what was going on. Michae
left the office. Stavros sat looking me up and down, his long
dark eyelashes and almost black eyes hardly moving.

'How old are you, Sandra?' he asked.

'Just turned twenty-one,' I said.

'You're a nice-looking girl,' he nodded. 'I hear you're
popular with the clients. You know how to talk to them.

112

That's good. I like a girl with brains who can talk,' he smiled. But it was not a friendly smile.

'You're coming with me tonight,' he went on. ' 'Cause I think you can do other things with that pretty mouth of yours.' He laughed, a horrible, dry cackle, which sent shivers down my back. I detested him from that moment on. I was shocked – no one had ever spoken to me like that before.

He looked back at the other man, who grinned.

I stared at Stavros, feeling cheap and dirty, lower than my street sisters who pounded the patch every night.

He stood up and cocked his head towards the door.

'Let's go,' he said.

The other man leapt across and opened the door for him. I followed him out. A chauffeur-driven Rolls-Royce was waiting at the entrance and we climbed in. We went to a sumptuous flat in Kensington – Stavros's town house, as he told me.

Once inside, he sent the other man away, and poured two whiskies, without asking me if I even liked Scotch. I sat on a fancy chrome and leather chair, feeling frightened. He settled down opposite on a matching couch.

He said nothing, just sipped at his whisky, looking at me with a horrible sneer on his face.

'Okay, little talker, let's see what you're made of,' he finally said. 'Get your clothes off.'

I started to get up to leave, but he jumped up and slapped me hard across the face. I fell to the floor, crying. He hauled me up with one hand, and with the other ripped my dress down the front.

'You do as I say,' he hissed into my face, his spittle spraying across my cheek. 'Or else. And there's no use in trying to scream. I'll stop you before your mouth is even open.'

I knew he meant it. Shaking I took my dress and bra off, and stood before him in my panties and stockings.

'Down on your knees, slut,' he leered, and pushed my shoulders down, forcing me to the floor.

He unzipped his trousers and pulled out his penis which was fully erect.

'Eat,' he sneered.

Tears pouring down my cheeks, I bent forward and took his penis in my mouth. He gripped my hair and pushed my head backwards and forwards. He climaxed in my mouth, painfully pressing my head against his stomach. I had to swallow.

He pulled my head away. I wanted to vomit.

'The bedroom,' he grunted, pointing to a door.

I was like a zombie as I walked across to the door. I pushed it open, and froze, too terrified to walk in. A huge round bed took up most of the room. It was covered with black silk sheets and a black sheepskin rug. The walls were completely mirrored and a round smoked glass mirror was fixed to the ceiling above the bed. Black fur rugs were scattered over the floor. But it was what lay on a small, round white table by the bed that made me so frightened. It was piled with whips, ropes and leather handcuffs.

Stavros came up behind, and pushed me into the bedroom, flinging me on the bed.

He stripped and picked up a small bull-whip.

'Turn around,' he muttered. 'On your stomach.'

I didn't move. He slapped me hard again and forced me round. The whip cracked noisily over my buttocks. I screamed into the covers, the stinging pain going through my whole body. He whipped me for about five minutes, after which I felt so raw and weakened I thought I would die.

He wasn't finished. He grabbed my arm and dragged me off the bed. I staggered to my feet, catching a glimpse of myself in the mirrors. My make-up had run down my face giving me black lines across my cheeks. I saw my back. Surprisingly my buttocks and lower back were not bleeding – they felt as if the skin had been torn off – but ugly red weals were striped across them.

Stavros gave me the whip and lay on his stomach on the bed.

'Come on,' he snarled. 'Hurry up!'

He wanted me to whip him! I was so exhausted, that I could hardly raise the whip. Oh, God, how I wished I'd had the strength to beat him to a pulp!

At each lash, he moaned and pushed himself into the bed.

hen his body became stiff as he climaxed over the sheets. stood limply, the whip in my hand. A wave of nausea came ver me and I rushed to his bathroom where I was violently ick. I was crying, my back felt as if it was on fire and my ody would not stop shaking. I wished I was dead.

'You can go now,' he muttered, when I staggered out. Michael'll pay you at the club. Oh, by the way,' he said, oking at me. 'You were good. Very good. You'll be with e for a while, y'hear? And don't do anything funny. And on't go out with anyone else. I don't want to catch the pox,' e laughed.

I nodded, too weak to even speak.

I didn't turn up to the club for a couple of days while y back healed. I went round to the agency to see if Stavros ad left instructions for me to be taken off the list. He hadn't, I assumed he didn't mean what he had said about not oing out with clients. What a mistake!

I was taken out by a shy little businessman from Man-hester. We went to L'Épée D'or in the Cumberland Hotel, nd then on to the club. Michael didn't say anything when I urned up, so again I thought everything was fine. We went ack to the John's hotel where I insisted he had to enter me om the rear, my back still being too painful for missionary-osition intercourse.

It was nearly one o'clock in the morning when I arrived ack at my flat. I was tired and depressed. I switched on e lights and had the shock of my life. Two dark-skinned en sat in the lounge. One I recognized as the man who had een with Stavros.

'What . . . what do you want?' I gasped.

They didn't answer. Instead, the man I hadn't seen before tood up, came across to me and grabbed my wrist, twisting y arm behind my back. Stavros's friend watched, his eyes its. He had on the same coat as he wore in Michael's office. oth men had on black leather gloves.

'What are you doing?' I cried.

The man holding me hit me across the mouth. I tasted lood.

Stavros's bodyguard (as I found out later) stood slowly

and strolled across. He was taller than me or the other man. He looked down at me.

'When Mr Stavros tells you not to go out with punks,' he said, 'you do as you're told.' He glanced at the other man. 'Bring her through.'

I struggled, but the man was too strong for me. I was pushed into my bedroom.

'What are you going to do?' I wept.

The bodyguard turned and slapped the back of his hand across my face.

'Shut up! Nikos, keep the fanny-peddler quiet,' he ordered the other man.

A gloved hand was pressed tightly across my mouth. I tried to bite him, but he laughed and hit the side of my head with his free hand. I was forced on to the bed and had my dress, bra and pants ripped off. The taller man pushed my legs open and knelt on my ankles, making it impossible for me to move.

'This is just a warning,' he sneered, pulling out a switchblade and flicking it open.

I screamed, but no sound came through the gloved hand on my mouth. I watched, horrified beyond belief, as he leant forward, and paused, the blade only about six inches away from my clitoris. He laid the edge of the knife on the inside of my thigh. Smiling like a maniac, he ran it along the soft skin for a few inches. I felt warm blood dripping down. He did this six times on one leg. And the same on the other.

I was past pain, past crying. My mind and body were numb. He moved up the bed and laid the bloodied blade under my left nipple and leered into my face. I felt the sticky blade against my breast and the thought of what he was going to do was too much for me. I passed out.

When I woke about an hour later, the pain in my thighs was agonizing. The bed was spattered, and my legs caked with blood. But my nipples were intact, thank God.

I washed, every dab of the disinfectant water like a hundred red-hot needles going through my thigh. I noticed a bottle of aspirin lying in the bathroom and toyed with it. I actually opened the top and spilled them out. It was the nearest I have ever come to suicide.

But I didn't even have the energy for that.

I crawled back to bed and eventually fell asleep. I was wakened by the telephone ringing in the middle of the next morning. It was Stavros.

'Can you come round to my place tonight?' he asked. 'I got a small party.'

'I can hardly move,' I told him.

'What? The boys do you in rough? I told you, baby, I told you. Well, if you're no good I'll get another whore for tonight. Get back to the club when you're fit. If you don't we'll come looking for you,' he said and hung up.

Another 'whore', he had said. But as I lay there weeping, I knew he was right. So much for my ideals. I *was* a whore, a thug's plaything. I was frightened, had nowhere to go. London's a big place, but the centre around Soho and Mayfair is a small world on its own. And I couldn't very well go back to the communes.

And so I did the only thing I could. I worked the club.

The whipping and sex with Stavros were nothing to what he made me do later. As soon as I went back to the club he called round and we went back to his place. But I won't – can't – talk about it. It was horrible. That beast indulged in every perversion.

I lost interest in everything. I did what he told me. Mechanically, with no feeling. I was his slave, and knew it. I began to drink heavily, something which Stavros encouraged. He would ply me with drink at his flat, and when I was almost too drunk to stand, he would start his filthy practices on me, laughing at my inability to stop him.

I don't know how I lived through those months. I made no attempt to get away. I knew it was useless. I was trapped. Stavros paid for my flat and gave me just enough money to exist. Sometimes he would send his friends round and they would abuse me in the same way as he did.

I knew Stavros would tire of me. I would probably end up on the bash (*street-walking* – ARR). I'd heard Stavros had a few girls on the street, controlled by pimps and his thugs. I met one of these girls. She was twenty-six, and looked about forty-two. Her face had a hard, emotionless look. And I'll never forget her eyes. They were dead. She'd lost all feeling, didn't care about life any more. She was on drugs (cocaine and junk, I think) which Stavros supplied. When I told her she'd be dead within two years, she just nodded.

I was looking at myself in a few years, I thought. But worse much worse, I didn't care.

The beatings, the constant humiliations did two things to me. Firstly I lost my self-respect. I wasn't a person, a thinking individual, but a whore of the worst sort, a piece of flesh to be used. No more. Secondly, I lost any ambitions I may have had after meeting Hath. There seemed no point. In anything. No point in going back to my friends in the communes where I'd be just as miserable; no point in going back to Scotland where nothing waited for me; no point in becoming an individual prostitute – if the girls didn't beat me up for encroaching on their patch, their pimps and muscle-men would.

As I say, I was completely trapped. I was just over twenty-one and felt my life was a total waste.

And then I met Roger Harringay. He came along to the agency one night because, he said, he 'needed some company'. I had been right about Stavros. He was seeing less of me, having found someone else. I was told to work the club and agency, which was at least a break from that brute.

Roger was about six feet tall, and looked the typical public school product. He was dressed in a sports suit and polo neck jumper when he came into the agency. His long, bony face was smooth, his short, black hair brushed straight back with a parting. The stereotype bourgeois, I thought. He's probably got a wife and three kids stashed away in the country like Hath.

But I was wrong. We ate at the Coq d'Or. Roger was nervous, not sure what to do. But after a few drinks he began to relax. 'I've never done this sort of thing before,' he told me. 'And I'm pleasantly surprised to find someone like you working in an agency.'

I nodded. They all said the same thing.

He was a merchant banker separated from his wife. He looked in his mid-thirties, and while not the most handsome of men, he was certainly presentable, as I think they say in the best circles.

I asked him why he came to the agency (something we normally didn't do, as clients often wouldn't admit they just wanted a bed-partner for the night).

'Surely you must know lots of *decent* women,' I said bitterly.

He laughed.

'Oh, I do, I do. But they're not my type.'

'Which is?'

'I don't know,' he said, his hazel eyes staring directly into mine. 'But I do know what I don't want – these blue-stockinged stuck-up bitches who think they're God's gift to men,' he sighed. 'I know what they're like. I was married to one.'

I laughed. And it was a genuine laugh. The first for months. And I ate a full meal, instead of just toying with the food. I had an absolutely huge Dover sole followed by fresh fruit salad. I hardly drank. I didn't feel I needed to.

Roger made me feel at ease. He spoke about this and that, treating me as someone intelligent, not just an object to take to bed as quickly as he could, which most clients wanted. I was beginning to feel human again.

I took him to the club where he laughed at having to buy two bottles of wine. 'I've heard of places like this,' he grinned. 'And I can't say I'm particularly impressed.'

He suggested coffee at the Hilton. Oh no, I thought, he *is* just like the others.

'Is that where you're staying?' I asked.

'Good God, no!' he laughed. 'I've got a house in Eton Square. But the Hilton's a lot better than this hole, if you don't mind me saying.'

I didn't and loved him for saying it.

At the Hilton, he was the perfect gentleman. Mannerly, courteous and he never once hinted at sex. I began to realize he had been serious when he said he only wanted company. He offered to run me home. But I couldn't move. The night had been so *normal*, I didn't want it to end.

Feeling heavy, I sat in his Jaguar saying nothing on the short ride back to my flat.

'Well, thank you very much for an enjoyable evening,' he said, going into his jacket pocket and pulling out his wallet. I felt terrible when I saw him take out some ten-pound notes.

'I don't want your money,' I said, my throat feeling tight. 'You've paid the agency. That's enough. I enjoyed the evening as well.'

He was obviously confused. And more confused when I suddenly burst out crying. I couldn't help it. For a few hours I'd managed to forget Stavros. When Roger said good-bye it all came back. No wonder I broke down.

He pulled me close, resting my head against his shoulder. 'What's wrong, Sandra?' he murmured. 'Tell me.'

I told him everything. Stavros, the club, what was happening to me. I did not mention Hath or my ideas of sexual class warfare. I gave him the facts. They were enough.

He said nothing for a few minutes. Then he started the car and began to drive off.

'We're going to my place,' he said calmly.

I said nothing. My mind was a blank. He led me gently into his flat. There was no suggestion of sex that night. I was too upset. He showed me the guest room and came back when I was in bed.

He looked down at me.

'I'm sorry,' I said, tears in my eyes.

'*You're* sorry!' he said angrily. 'God, people like Stavros shouldn't be allowed to exist!' he fumed, and then smiled. 'But it's over now. Get some sleep,' he said, bending over and kissing me on the forehead.

I hardly slept between crying and wondering what was going to happen. I couldn't believe that anyone could be so generous, especially after what I'd been through. And I also dreaded the morning. Would Roger change his mind? Things always look different in the cold light.

But he came in at 7.30 am with a cup of tea for me.

'If you feel up to it,' he said, sitting on the edge of the bed, looking young in his pyjamas and dressing gown, 'we'll get across to your flat and pick up your things now. Before that bastard realizes you're missing.'

'Where will I go?' I asked. I was taking no chances, taking nothing for granted.

'You're moving in here, silly,' he grinned. 'Where did you think?'

I put the cup down and hugged him. There was no hint of anything but gratitude in my hug, and he knew it. It was the sort of thing I would have done to a brother.

But what happened in the following weeks and months made me forget family feeling. For I found out that, as expected, Roger's generosity had a price . . .

It began one night after an absolutely super dinner at L'Ambassadeur. I'd been with Roger for about three weeks. We were making love by this time, of course. Nothing special – just normal, straightforward, gentle intercourse. And I loved it. He was good in bed, didn't rush and gave me satisfaction. I was happy. But I wouldn't go out alone, in case I ran into Stavros or his henchmen.

Roger had been modest when he said he was 'only a merchant banker'. He was very successful and friendly with wealthy, influential and famous people. He was on first-name terms with many film stars and singers, often handling financial matters for them. And without any embarrassment or feelings of shame, he introduced me to them. These were good days. Very good days.

But that night it all changed. We'd had two bottles of champagne and I was giggling like a schoolgirl as we drove home. Roger insisted on having another drink before going to bed, although the state I was in all I wanted was to grab him and tear the clothes off him!

We sat in the tastefully, but not ostentatiously, furnished front room, brandies in our hands. Roger was opposite me. I was wearing a two-piece Cardin suit he'd bought me, and I could see he kept glancing at the tops of my stockings as he spoke, something he didn't normally do.

'Darling,' he said, 'what sort of things did you do to your

customers at the agency?'

I stiffened. This was the first time he had mentioned my past.

'I don't want to talk about it,' I said. 'It's over and done with.'

'I'd like you to talk about it. I'm interested,' he smiled. 'Why?'

'I'm just curious, that's all.'

I couldn't really see the harm and so told him about some of the kinkier clients. The men who wanted threesomes; men who wanted me to dress up or dress them up; and then I described in more accurate detail what I'd gone through with Stavros.

'I think it's amazing that the most respectable-looking men can be so warped,' I ended up by saying.

Roger stretched his long legs out and, half-closing his eyes, looked at me with a strange smile on his lips.

'I don't think anything that gives pleasure should be sneered at,' he said quietly.

'What if it hurts?' I asked, beginning to realize the conversation had a point to it. One I didn't want to follow through.

'Oh, that's wrong,' he nodded. 'Both people should want to do whatever it is. And if they do agree, you can't say it hurts if it gives them pleasure.'

I didn't answer for a few seconds.

'Do you like any of the things I've been talking about?' putting my feelings into words.

'Some of them, yes. But not what that animal Stavros did to you. That's really sick.'

'Would you . . . would you like me to play some of the games with you?'

He didn't give me a direct answer, but stood up and led me through to the bedroom. Taking a key from his pocket, he opened a wall cupboard. Inside was a complete range of sex toys and clothes! Cloaks, hoods, handcuffs, whips, and spanking paddles. A whole series of vibrators, all different shapes and sizes, were lined neatly along a shelf.

'My private collection,' he said proudly, as if showing me some rare paintings.

We were beginning to sober up, so Roger went into the kitchen for another bottle of champagne. The night was only beginning for him, obviously, although it was nearly one in the morning.

While he was out of the room. I went through the cupboard. I quickly slipped out of my suit, and put on a pair of thigh-length leather boots, an eye-mask and picked up a whip. I thought I looked like something out of these sex comics I'd seen. But Roger, when he came back, reacted quite differently.

'That's fantastic,' he grunted.

I could see he had an enormous erection. I cracked the whip on the bed. How far would the game go? I wondered. I still had on my bra, panties, suspenders and black stockings. Roger fell to his knees and began to kiss my vagina through the thin material of my panties.

I became excited, but pushed him away.

'Now, now,' I said. 'You can't do that yet. You didn't ask me. You'll have to be punished for being rude.'

He quickly stripped and I led him across to the bed before making him lie on his stomach.

'This is for being a bad boy,' I said, bringing the whip down across his buttocks. He moaned and squirmed slightly. I went on hitting him for about five minutes. Not too hard, as I'd tried to do with Stavros, but just enough to make him feel the tingling over his back. When I finished his buttocks and part of his back were bright red. (This disappeared overnight and in the morning there was no trace of the whip – a cat-o'-nine-tails with soft leather thongs – on his back.)

He turned over, his penis throbbing almost with a life of its own.

'Now put me inside you,' he said gutturally.

I stood on the bed, my legs to either side of him. Slowly I lowered myself into a squatting position, his penis touching the lips of my vagina. I was excited, and ready for him. But I slid down slowly, feeling him enter me, savouring every second, enjoying his hardness pressing against my warmth, my nerves alive to each change of pressure. I moved my hips round and round, the sensations deep inside of me making me moan as well. We climaxed together, waves of emotion spreading from my stomach up to my throat. I was sweating, breathless and exhausted.

Later as we lay on the bed completely naked, my body heavy with pleasant tiredness, he turned and stroked my hair. 'Thanks,' he said simply.

'No, my love, thank you,' I said, meaning it.

Over the past few weeks, Roger had managed to reawaken my sexual awareness, something which had almost been destroyed by the agency and Stavros. And believe me, I was very grateful for this. And if Roger wanted me to dress up and excite him with whips and spanking paddles, then I would do it.

After all, he *had* saved my life . . .

As time went by, Roger's sexual demands became more and more bizarre. I had to tie him down on the bed, put a tight corset on, and spank him even before he was aroused. Often he would watch me masturbate with one of the vibrators. One of his favourite turn-ons was to be tied to the corners of the bed, spreadeagled. I then had to kneel in front of him and perform oral sex on him. And *then*, after that, I would have to whip him and make love sitting on top of him.

To begin with, I enjoyed the games as much as he did. But then I seemed to change. I wasn't getting as much out of the sex-play as I should have, I thought. I daren't mention this to Roger, of course. He was so kind in every other way, and I felt gratitude – I still do – for what he had done for me.

As each day passed, I became more confident about Stavros not finding me. (I found out much later that a few months after I'd disappeared, a girl whom he was using pulled a knife from her stocking top one night and slashed it through his erect penis, castrating him. I felt jealous of her courage, but not after I heard what had been done to her. She had been horribly tortured, and then killed, parts of her body being dumped over Soho. Her head has never been found.)

I began thinking of the old days before Stavros. My

revolutionary beliefs, my old friends like Alec, what I had set out to do after my experience with Hath. And then one morning, while I was lying in bed, it suddenly struck me that Roger was one of the very class I had sworn revenge against! I began to laugh, thinking how crazy it all was! There I was, living in the lap of luxury, having nothing to do but keep Roger sexually satisfied, in the very position I'd dreamed about for years!

And if I didn't get the same thrills out of sex as he did, wasn't this because his weaknesses, or perversions, were a basic hereditary malfunction of his class? Of course!

So a new excitement, a different sort of pleasure, began to fill me as I whipped and humiliated him. Roger, of course, never noticed the difference. In fact, he never once asked me what *I* felt about our sexual deviations. If I had an orgasm, that was good enough for him. And I knew how to pretend, just to please him, even when I experienced nothing.

I don't think what I felt was that important to him. *He* was getting what he wanted. And I had no illusions. Once he tired of our little games, he would be out on the hunt again, looking for new blood. I started to collect the names, addresses and private phone numbers from most of the wealthy, influential and famous people I was introduced to through Roger.

However, once the amusement wore off, I began to see myself as a hypocrite. Here I was, pandering to my own needs and the sexual fantasies of a leading financier, while millions were suffering throughout the world because of people like Roger. I saw myself as a Dr Jekyll and Mr Hyde character. Mr Hyde enjoyed going to the Dorchester for dinner, to the Grosvenor for balls, to the Ritz for caviar and to parties in the homes of the wealthy. Dr Jekyll felt pain and shame at what the other half of me was doing. He wanted to compensate for my hypocrisy by helping down-trodden victims of the system. And it was during one of my Dr Jekyll periods that I phoned some of my old friends on *International Times* and arranged to meet them at a pub in Islington.

I turned up wearing denims, an old loose-fitting jumper and sneakers. My hair was tied in a ribbon at the back and I wore hardly any make-up. I took the Tube to Islington, although I always had the use of Roger's Jag when I needed it. I didn't want any of my old friends to know what sort of life-style I was following. In a strange way, you see, I was ashamed.

They were all there. The same old faces, the same old outfits, the same old ideas. They didn't quiz me as to what I had been doing, which I appreciated. A bottle or two of wine was drunk, and as I travelled back on the Tube that afternoon I felt relaxed, happy and more balanced.

As I was leaving, Alec took me by the arm.

'It's all happening now, baby,' he said. 'We gotta lot of action moving. The forces are uniting. It's a good time to be with the movement.'

'I was never out of it,' I smiled.

We arranged to meet every week and I started going along to a few aggro meetings in Islington organized by Trotsky-ists and Maoists. A new type of activist was appearing around 1968, the year of the Student Revolt in Paris. They were younger, more eager and somehow more intellectual, I thought. And most of them seemed to come from middle-class backgrounds. Alec was right. It was a good time.

The new activists (as well as the old, of course), were sickened by Vietnam, thrilled about Che Guevara, and saw Americans as the present-day imperialists, using the same techniques of torture and terror the British and French had used.

We talked a lot about the Third World, I remember. How America, backed by Britain, was trying to destroy the New Wave of awareness. Capitalism had an ally now – colonialism. These two were the twin forces of evil, and it was up to us, the new revolutionaries, to put an end to them. And our actions would make the people aware. For hadn't Mao called his guerillas 'Fish swimming in the sea of the people'? We were the fish, and it was vital we did not cut ourselves off.

Applied to my own situation, which I never mentioned, this philosophy gave me a logical basis for the way I was living. My dedication to the class struggle was re-affirmed. Instead of the bullets used by my comrades in South America and Vietnam, I was using my body to help destroy capitalism and those that supported it . . .

But to do this, I had to be on my own. I couldn't do much in the pretend world Roger had created for me. I told the dear man I thought it was time I moved out – 'to give you a chance to lead your life without me hanging round your neck.' Of course I would see him in the future. He took it well, and I still think in a way he was glad to be rid of me. Like all men, he liked change!

He was *so* kind, I almost found it embarrassing. He helped me find, and partly paid for, a flat in Farm Street, Mayfair. It was perfect – near to the Dorchester, the Hilton and The Inn on the Park. Places I knew I would be visiting. For by now I had a very impressive list of names in my book.

Surely, surely, I could do something positive at last? I had been through hell and come out of it. I was lucky, and never forgot it. I was also tougher, more wary than before. Ready for my new class battles, I felt. But it was to take nearly two years before I began fighting in earnest. Before then, I was to discover that household names and personalities could cause as much misery and suffering in their own way as the thugs and crooks I'd escaped.

CHAPTER 9

At the start, business at the massage parlour was slow. Mikhail lost his normal, cool approach on a few occasions, claiming the parlour was a waste of time.

'All these things take time, sweetheart,' Sandra would tell him, smiling and shaking her head. 'The reputation has got to be built up. You'll see what I mean.'

Which is what did happen, in fact. Gradually, a regular clientele built up over the months and the parlour after four months was showing a healthy profit. Mikhail apologized to Sandra, and told her he would leave all such arrangements up to her in the future. But because of the pressure he was under from Prague and Moscow, he always interfered. Sandra found his questions irritating at first, then amusing. During their arguments, she would put on a sexy voice and slink over to him, rubbing the back of his neck with her fingers.

'Now you're not going to start telling me off again, are you, darling?' she would purr, blinking her eyes innocently.

It always worked. Mikhail would smile, and Sandra would get her own way. But she was not so stupid as to think she was not being watched, studied and being accounted for in offices from the Czech Embassy in London to the KGB Headquarters in Moscow. And she gave reasons for everything she did, from recruiting a new girl to buying equipment. The Russians, who seemed to have an obsession with well-balanced accounts, were delighted, which meant the Czechs were also pleased.

Sandra was never to know just how much money she could spend, but knew it was always there when she needed it. Once the various set-ups became profitable, like the massage parlour, she did not use the floating fund so often.

What particularly pleased Sandra about the massage parlour was that it was beginning to attract the sort of people the STB had in mind as targets. It was not the type of club visited by day trippers and tourists. After the first month, she introduced membership cards, making it more exclusive. And the front was improved upon, which meant if a suspecting wife ever found the membership card, and visited the parlour, all she would see were well-dressed young ladies and innocent cubicles with no hint of smut.

Civil servants began to use the parlour's facilities as well as businessmen. It was open from ten in the morning until ten at night, and at any given time during the day there was always at least one man being 'attended to'.

When Sandra was satisfied things were going smoothly, she moved on to the next stage – the setting up of an escort agency.

She had learnt well while with Stavros's agency. She had seen that the only reason it seemed to do well was because of its location. But that had its drawbacks also, she realized, because it tended to attract a lot of foreign visitors who stayed in the many hotels around Marble Arch – not the people she was interested in. And she also knew most of the girls who went into the escort business were only one stage away from pounding the streets.

'What we need,' she told Mikhail, 'is a more sophisticated operation. We've got to get a higher class of girl if we want a better class of man.'

'I agree,' Mikhail nodded. 'But where do we get them?'

Sandra smiled.

'Air hostesses are always looking for extra money and tend to be polished and suave. We'll use them for the agency.'

Over the next month, Sandra travelled to Switzerland and back twice a week. She began to know some of the hostesses, but did not discuss the agency with them. These trips were to collect operational data for use later. She became familiar with the jargon of hostesses, their grumbles and moans, and how they operated in the air. By the end of the month, she was able to pass herself off as an ex-hostess. Then she began recruiting.

Taking different airlines to various parts of Europe, she began talking to the girls about how things had changed since her day, and the pay did not seem to be that much better. When they asked her what she was doing, she said she was running a small escort agency which, for very little work, brought in a lot of money for her and her girls. Sandra left a card with each girl, and told them to be in touch should they ever fancy a change.

After two months, she had twelve air hostesses on her books. After that, it was word of mouth as the girls would tell their friends how easy it was to pick up extra money for doing next to nothing. And Sandra was generous. She gave the girls thirty per cent of the fee (£20) and allowed them to keep any 'presents' clients gave them. Which meant that by the time the agency entered its third month, she had nearly fifty girls to call on at any one time. As soon as the hostesses landed they phoned the office and were put on the active list.

And the good reputation worked the other way. Clients were pleasantly surprised by the standard of the girls and soon the agency had a regular clientele which was expanding rapidly as word spread.

The agency itself was situated in Regent Street, below a jazz club. This location was found by Sandra, again after a lot of legwork. What made it ideal was that the music club and the agency shared a common entrance. Once past swing doors, however, there were two more doors, the one on the left leading up some stairs to the agency. So it always appeared as if clients were entering the jazz club, which was very popular anyway.

A uniformed commissionaire sat in a small hall on the landing outside the agency, during the hours it was open. No one was allowed past until he had phoned through to reception to see if the client was expected.

Once inside, the client found himself in what looked like the luxurious front parlour of a country house. Wall-to-wall carpeting, hessian wallpaper and rows of antique prints of London on the walls gave the impression of comfort. Two leather Chesterfield couches in front of a Victorian coffee able added to the feeling. An antique gilt desk was provided or the receptionist; two telephones stood on it. A red internal phone and a white external. No girls were to be seen hanging round, Sandra insisted, as it 'would make the place look like Chinese brothel'.

Rooms led off the reception area, which served as changing and dressing rooms for the girls. There was even a bedroom should a girl want to stay the night. Under no circumstances were the girls to invite clients into the bedroom, as this would be infringing the local laws which dealt with prostitution and they could be rightly accused of running a brothel.

The client would wait in reception while piped music (again classical) played softly in the background. Some of them would wander round the room studying the prints. Not one of them would realize that two of the prints, those near the ceiling, had hidden cameras behind, operated from two small rooms behind false walls.

Sandra recruited Meg Thomson, a girl she had known from her days in the other agency, as receptionist. Meg was intelligent, always smartly dressed, and completely trustworthy. And she would never cross Sandra. When Sandra contacted her with the offer, Meg was in desperate financial trouble over some medical bills. Sandra paid them immediately, not wanting the money back, saying that's what friends are for. In fact she was buying Meg's loyalty.

Once the girls had been recruited and the premises furnished, Sandra had started doing the rounds of the top hotels. She knew that the best public relations was the spoken word and that at the many conferences held in hotels, men almost inevitably asked the hotel porters for advice about places to visit, either discreetly or not.

Sandra had some difficulty at first with the head porters. They had a hundred cards, they claimed, from escort agencies and what was different about hers? She gave all the usual answers about a better type of girl and service, but they were not convinced. Finally she pointed out that if a client came to the agency on their recommendation, they would receive £5 for each man. Now that *was* different, they all said. And Sandra's agency began to be visited by top businessmen, wealthy foreigners (who only helped bring in extra cash, as far as she was concerned), and even the occasional MP as word spread.

After that, the agency was self-perpetuating. Sandra soon discovered an escort agency was big business and more satisfactory than regular call-girl services 'in the same way that Woolworths is better business than Harrod's or Fortnum & Mason's', as she put it.

Sandra again chose the name. Mikhail laughed when he heard it, given the type of girls who worked in it. She called it 'The Top Flight Agency'.

It had taken six months to set up the massage parlour and agency. Sandra felt they were moving slowly, but Mikhail seemed to be pleased. He could see and understand what she was doing, and did not complain. And, more important, the men in Prague and Moscow seemed pleased also.

At this point Mikhail introduced Sandra to George, an East End Londoner. George was small, dressed fairly well, and had sandy-coloured hair which was blow-waved at the front in the style of the 1950s. He always had a quip or a joke ready for every occasion. Sandra took to him immediately and they had a mutually adoring relationship of the sort sometimes found between a master and his dog, or between people from opposite ends of the social scale.

George was one of those men always found floating through the underworld in all the major capitals of the world. He was well-known to many of the pimps and prostitutes around Soho and Mayfair. He knew where to procure almost any item Sandra, or anyone else, needed. And he was trusted. In his mid-forties, George told Sandra he had been living on his wits since the age of sixteen. Never once had he given the police any information which could have led to arrests, although he knew about almost every major crime that took place in London. Because of his easy-going manner he was accepted by nearly all of those who make up the grey, twilight world.

Sandra never found out what his connection with Mikhail was, and why he worked for the Czechs. And George never asked what she was doing. They had a good working relationhip, and their respectful admiration for each other was an added bonus.

Mikhail also organized a team of strong-arm men. Sandra protested about this, saying she did not need any protection of this sort. Mikhail laughed when she complained.

'We're not protecting *you*, Sandra,' he said. 'We're protecting the operation. You're going to have a lot of strange people approaching you in the next few months. Some will be straight, but others will be connected with the vice gangs. We've got to show we're as strong as them when it comes to using their methods. And also,' he added, 'should someone be a little slow about making up their minds over any payment or coming into the network, we can persuade them otherwise,' he smiled.

The muscle-men took their orders directly from Mikhail. And they did exactly as they were told. The STB threatened to expose the fact that they were illegal immigrants from the Balkans if they disobeyed.

But the STB knew that any operation of the magnitude they had in mind – and even Sandra did not know the full details as yet – could not depend on brute force alone. A 'Mr Big', as Mikhail jokingly called him, was brought in to back up Sandra, George and the team of protectors. Mr Big, or Watson, was a leading Establishment figure who sat on the boards of many charities. Watson used influence in the same way as the team of muscle-men used muscle.

Watson was in his sixties, a distinguished-looking man with grey hair and a strong, impressive face. He was under long-standing blackmail pressure from the STB – again, Sandra never found out exactly what for, but she knew Mikhail provided him with a rare drug he needed in return for his services.

What was happening, though Mikhail never explained this to Sandra at any time, was that as the network expanded and became stronger, the 'administration' of the overt operation was being strengthened also. Mikhail and his bosses realized it was impossible for one person to control the whole system. Sandra was becoming the figurehead at the top of a powerful and influential team. The Czechs were taking no chances. For what they had in mind was too big, too important, for any slip-ups.

The appearance of George, Watson and the muscle-men frightened Sandra, for two reasons. Firstly, she knew she could not get out of the operation, even if she wanted. They wouldn't let her. And secondly, she was becoming aware that the operation was larger than she had imagined at first. Just how large, she had no idea. But when she did find out, it frightened her even more.

The network expanded rapidly. Individual girls were recruited to help compile the catalogue. Sandra and George spent weeks scouring London for suitable girls who specialized in 'discipline', orgies, group sex, and the many sexual deviations to be found on any advertising board in Soho. The girls were interviewed by George first and then Sandra. They were not chosen at random. They were approached on George's recommendation.

After a month, they had fifty girls working indirectly for them, from a girl who picked up men in a pub in Soho to a 'loner' who worked the gambling clubs. George dealt mainly with the pimps, giving them enough money regularly to keep them quiet and loyal. He did the same with the pushers, the men who actively tout for prostitutes. In return, the girls had to pass on information about any man they thought was important and report his particular sexual deviation.

Not one of the girls, pimps or pushers had any idea they were part of a network which effectively covered central London.

Sandra managed to bribe some girls in other massage parlours to pass on information. Every day she would receive some piece of news. Most of it was useless, but occasionally a name would crop up and be entered in the catalogue.

The catalogue was simply compiled. Mikhail supplied a long list of names of leading businessmen, politicians, civil servants and public figures. Should any man on that list appear within the network, he was entered into a catalogue. Nothing might be done for years, in some cases, but when necessary, he could be compromised in an operation, using the information from the catalogue.

One of the richest sources for entries were the porn-shops in Soho. Between them, George and Sandra expanded this vital area.

Specially trained KGB and STB agents were put into the most popular shops. These men, who were always British, had been trained to recognize many of the people on the target list. The STB had used this technique for years. Sandra and George only refined it. By the time they were finished, every shop with a large turnover as well as those specializing in under-the-counter sales, had an STB agent in it. And they were all providing information on an almost daily basis.

Mikhail supplied two 'clerks' from the Embassy to help Sandra and himself sift through the mass of material that was beginning to flow in.

But the network was not yet complete. Loopholes had to be plugged, and the whole net upgraded. Sandra, who was still seeing clients, became a madam, controlling a small team of a dozen girls who catered exclusively to the wealthy and influential.

She chose each girl herself. Six of them she had known from the old days, and were those she had helped when they were in trouble. As with Meg, she had not realized at the time that she was buying loyalty, but when she began to operate her own ring, she found these girls completely trustworthy. Under no circumstances would they break the very high code of honour which exists between working girls at a certain level.

The rest of the girls she approached after hearing of their reputations. Some specialized in whipping or torture; others provided threesome sex; one girl pandered to urinologists and yet another was a great favourite with the wealthy Arabs because of her expertise in anal sex.

Sandra would meet them in Fortnum & Mason's tea shop at first. After some light chat, she would offer the girls a deal. Sandra would buy a complete outfit of clothes and sex aids if necessary for the girls.

This could cost up to £1,000, to be paid back over a few

months. Some girls declined the offer, having adequate wardrobes already. Sandra had worked out a table of fees for the girls. For an afternoon date it was £40 an hour, and Sandra took £10 of this. An evening dinner and whatever followed, cost £60, of which £15 went back to Sandra.

Under no circumstances were the girls allowed to give clients their telephone numbers. All bookings went through Sandra, who normally saw the girls about once a week to collect her commission.

Looks were important. At the prices Sandra was working on, clients would expect exactly what they wanted. From her own experience she knew some men could only be aroused by a blonde wearing a leather mini-skirt, for example.

'It takes all kinds,' she would say. 'And we've got to cater to every taste.'

With the addition of the call-girl ring, the network was in a healthy financial position. Mikhail told her it was almost self-financing, a fact which particularly pleased the Russians.

But there were still loopholes. While prostitution in London is controlled largely by three or four gangs, it was still possible as Sandra was discovering to be an independent agent. At a price. There were two threats to her independence. The protection rackets that are part of the organized vice syndicate. And the police.

The protection rackets were simple to deal with. George and Watson kept them away. Should they become insistent, the muscle-men were called in. If that proved fruitless, Mikhail would arrange for some 'wet work' experts to be brought in from abroad. These men were trained killers who used sophisticated techniques of murder invented by the Soviets. Sandra never enquired about the work and Mikhail did not mention it. She only knew the threats always stopped.

Sandra, however, dealt directly with the police. Apart from not wanting to raise suspicions about her involvement with the Czechs, Sandra had known corrupt policemen ever since becoming a call-girl. As the network grew, it became necessary to pull in more and more policemen. Not for the occasional tip-off about raids, which was not worth the money as Sandra's establishments were always run along apparently legit lines, but again for protection. The police would keep her 'clean' by putting pressure on other gangsters.

Such protection did not come cheaply – as the organization expanded, payments to the police became the single largest item of expenditure. The Czechs paid up without complaint. For the police were not only safeguarding the network, they were in a roundabout way contributing to its success, as Sandra was to find out. A well-timed, pre-planned raid could do more for blackmail purposes than a thousand feet of incriminating film.*

Feathermucking, Sandra was discovering, was a highly sophisticated and challenging new profession. And one in which she was teaching the Czechs a few tricks along the way.

Sandra had been working on the network for nearly nine months. Only two more gaps remained to be filled – a club and a country house were needed. The club was found in Bruton Street, off Grosvenor Square, in a basement. This time Sandra personally supervised the decoration and furnishing.

In a basement, the club contained a small restaurant and dance floor. A three-piece combo played nightly. Drinks were expensive – a bottle of champagne cost £30, and the hostesses were specially picked for their beauty. Topless barmaids wearing fish-net stockings and suspender belts served behind a long bar. They never mixed with customers.

If a client wanted to speak with a girl, it cost him £10; if he took her back to his hotel, two bottles of champagne had to be bought. The average price of a girl was £50 for a visit to a client's hotel, £100 for the night. It was expensive. Deliberately so. Within a short time, some of the wealthiest

---

* There has been a great deal of talk and publicity about 'corrupt' policemen over the past few years, especially concerning those working in the London area. It is true that some policemen are genuinely 'bent', but there is not the widespread corruption generally believed to exist. In fact, most 'corruptible' policemen only *act* as if they are on the take and are doing so on instructions. If these policemen do not come forward at trials it is either because they are in danger of being killed or because as *agents provocateurs* their evidence is questionable. It is also a fact that one of the intelligence service's main methods of staying informed about developments in the world of vice and crime is through 'corrupt' policemen.

men in the country were visiting it. Two lords appeared within three months of it opening.

New techniques in bugging were being used. Instead of a still camera, small television cameras were used, four being placed in strategic spots round the club. Everything that went on in the club was video-taped for future use. The whole process was controlled from a small room at the back of the wine store. There was no entrance from the store itself, but from an alley at the side of the club not overlooked by anything, and where the dustbins were kept.

It was a perfect set-up. Sandra received a gold bracelet from Mikhail as a sign of his gratitude and admiration.

Four out of the twenty hostesses as well as the manageress in the club were 'swallows' who had trained in Russia and been in Britain for a few years. They knew all the tricks of feathermucking but did not have the 'class of Sandra' as Mikhail put it. One of the girls went round nightly with a camera, and if a target was in the club, would photograph him, surrounded by girls, including at least one swallow. The film went the same way as the Freddy Mallette drop, the only difference being that the John was given a copy to allay any suspicions.

The final hole in the net was plugged when Sandra rented a country house in Kent, about an hour and a half's drive from London. The house stood in five acres of its own grounds, and was approached by a long drive. Built in the nineteenth century, it had five large rooms on the ground floor, including a ballroom. The other two floors contained twelve bedrooms. The ballroom was converted into a gambling den with roulette, black-jack and poker. The bedrooms were completely redecorated and furnished with cameras and monitors.

The house had been used in the past by politicians and visiting heads of state. Sandra would use it for week-end parties, conferences and the Big Kill.

In less than a year a complete, almost watertight network stretched across London. From girls walking the streets to private parties, Sandra could have information for the catalogue within hours. Each unit appeared separate. Yet if someone on the list wanted to use an accommodation address, this would be passed back to Sandra and Mikhail. The man who answered an ad in a contact magazine for 'Fancy Dress Parties' and who turned out to be a transvestite would be entered in the catalogue. Look-outs in porn shops would lead Johns on with promises of hot stuff; if anyone on the list lost heavily at gambling clubs he would be approached by an STB principal agent.

The vice world of London had a nebulous thread running through it which led through many twists and turns to Sandra and Mikhail.

The amount of information being gathered was staggering. And yet not once was blackmail overtly used. The aim of the operation was to expose. Mikhail insisted that on no account should anyone attempt anything as crude as petty, direct blackmail, which would ruin their ultimate objective.

And so the orgies were staged, the photographs taken, the targets' involvements made deeper*, the catalogue constantly brought up to date and more targets added.

There were twenty-two leading civil servants in the net; seven Members of Parliament from all three parties and forty-one top businessmen. But still Mikhail would not give the go-ahead for the Big Kill. One final move had to be made. And only Sandra could make it.

Mikhail called her to the Hampstead safe-house one afternoon. He looked excited, pacing around the room, his eyes hard and bright.

'Wonderful,' he muttered, as Sandra sat down and lit a cigarette. 'We can move into the final stages now. Wonderful.'

Sandra looked up expectantly at him.

'The big one,' he said, stopping in front of her. 'The one we've been waiting for. Your biggest fish and the one that completes the catch. You'll have to forget everything else and concentrate on dropping him.'

Sandra sensed the tension in his voice.

'Who is it?' she asked.

'Lord Kingwood,' Mikhail replied excitedly. 'He's in the net.'

* Sandra describes these in detail later.

Sandra was stunned. Kingwood was a leading crusader against 'sin and pornography'. He had headed two commissions on pornography, was a household name and had become identified with every movement, cranky or otherwise, against permissiveness. He had been an MP, a member of the Cabinet, a QC and a judge. It was his economic policy which was still followed in part by the then Labour Government. Sandra found it almost impossible to believe he had been spotted in the net.

'Where was he seen?' she asked.

'A swingers' party,' Mikhail answered. 'You know, the private type. A dozen people, most of them on our target list, getting together for an evening. There was a live show with two Danish lesbians.'

'Incredible. Kingwood. I still can't believe it,' Sandra muttered. She frowned. 'But he has an out. He could always say he was investigating for his commissions. Everyone would believe him.'

Mikhail shook his head.

'In Dick Longman's country house? No, it was a set-up party and he went along willingly. I'm sure of it.'

'Has he been spotted since?'

'No, but we checked through our records and found that, on his raids on Soho bookshops, lesbian books were always taken away.'

'Proves nothing,' Sandra said, inhaling on her cigarette.

'That's what we thought,' Mikhail agreed. 'Until now. It's up to you to turn Kingwood's fantasies into reality.'

Sandra breathed in deeply.

'It's impossible. Absolutely impossible,' she said, shaking her head.

Mikhail's face hardened, and his eyes narrowed.

'It's not. We'll get him,' he said, staring at Sandra.

He was right. Within four months Kingwood was ready for the Big Kill.

CHAPTER 10

I was out on my own again, thanks to Roger. I had no illusions about myself. I'd been through too much to think I was going to set the world on fire or start a second Russian Revolution. I was a call-girl, a prostitute, a whore – call it what you will, I don't mind. For I had discovered that sex seemed to be the only common link between the classes. Every man, no matter what his job, class or position in life, wanted sex. And the married ones were the worst. Of course, I blame the wives, but let's not digress.

And anyway, I enjoy sex. I know all this stuff about a prostitute being as cold as a fish and so on. It's not true at the level I was working on. There were many occasions where I reached orgasm during intercourse with clients. Why? Because I was not a ten-pound lay. The men I dealt with paid well for something more than a two-minute release. Not all of them wanted to be beaten or whipped, many just liked straight intercourse without any strings attached. And I challenge any woman to go through an hour's foreplay with the man performing oral sex on her not to become excited!

I began to enjoy the 'games' also, seeing them as amusing. Many working girls I know have no sense of humour, and they become bitter about what they're doing. And it shows. They gradually lose their clients, end up in the street, become more bitter and finish up God knows where. You've got to see the funny side of it, I think, or you'll go mad.

I changed my name. Sandra Brown *sounds* so working class, after all. And with the names in my book, the men I hoped to meet and the circles I would be moving in, I wanted to be accepted on equal terms. I became Rochelle Duvalle.

This didn't present any problems, as far as the people

Roger had introduced to me were concerned. Given the average person's memory for names, they would assume they were wrong when they called me Sandra. And that's what happened. Rochelle Duvalle soon became well-known around the jet-setting circles of Mayfair and Belgravia. Roger, thinking the whole thing hilarious, promised to keep the secret.

The invitations began to flow when it became known I was on my own. And I made sure it became known! I spent three days on the phone, calling every number in my book. Soon my ex-directory private number was finding its way into the notebooks of the famous and wealthy. I knew at least six men in Hollywood had my number.

Film stars, pop singers, producers and business tycoons would phone me up and ask me out to parties, shows, trips down the Thames by yacht and week-end parties in the country. I was genuinely thrilled! It's not every girl who can say she's had J..... G..... whimpering in front of her, begging to be spanked. When I see him on television now, with his strong manly image, his shirt open to the waist, showing off his hairy chest and singing romantic songs, I still laugh. Especially as I know he's wearing a chest wig!

I loved being seen with them, pretending not to notice the heads turn in restaurants and clubs when we walked in. Who wouldn't want to be escorted by B..... S....., one of the world's most famous singers? The fact that I would find out later, that despite the largest record sales in the country he also had the smallest penis I'd ever seen, didn't really matter.

I was there! Me! Little Sandra Brown from the Gorbals. Mixing with the great. And my revolutionary friends? My ideals? Well, to be honest, I was enjoying myself so much I forgot them most of the time. My weekly attendances at meetings became fortnightly and then monthly. At times, however, I would have a pang of conscience and anonymously send along a few hundred pounds to some left-wing movement.

But please, don't get me wrong. I still *felt* for the cause. But what use was knowing that W..... T....., the film star, used erection cream to keep himself going through intercourse, to the struggle for the oppressed masses? That he always kept the cream in a silver box shaped like a Saint Christopher medallion round his neck would have made the Sunday papers. It would have hardly started a revolution!

Blackmail at that level never entered my head. My mind just was not into it. It was the same as before – give the papers a story, pick up a few hundred pounds, and then what? It wasn't worth it.

At the time, I enjoyed the jet-setting life, the gifts and the presents of money. For apart from going out with the famous, I was building my career on straight call-girl work. And learning all the time. Which was just as well, because what happened next finished me with jet-setters and the *nouveau riche*, who make up about ninety per cent of the music and film world, for ever.

P . . . . . N . . . . . had been my idol for years. I can remember standing in long queues in Glasgow to see his latest films, many of which I saw about four times. He was given my number by D . . . . . M . . . . . , who recommended me highly.

N . . . . . was an extrovert, and success had only brought out the worst in him. Born in London, he had gone to Hollywood when he was sixteen to become the internationally famous star he is now. On our first night out, we went back to his rented flat in Mayfair, where he pulled out a cardboard box.

'Open it,' he said, slurring slightly. We had just come from the Beachcomber, where he had lost a few thousand dollars on the gambling tables. We'd drunk two bottles of champagne and he'd had countless whiskies on top of that.

Inside the box was a nurse's uniform.

'Put it on,' he said.

The uniform was a little tight, and came to above my knees. As I had my stockings and suspenders on this thrilled him even more. We went through to the bedroom where he stripped.

'Now give me an enema,' he demanded, pointing at a rubber sac with a long tube leading out of it.

'*What*?' I asked. It was the strangest request I'd had to date. (Nothing to what I was asked to do later, mind you!)

He patiently explained what he wanted done. So I did it. And only *then* did he become aroused, and we had intercourse. He gave me $600 so I couldn't complain really. After that, it was always the same. Enema first – and he would supply a whole series of them – and then intercourse. I drew the line when he asked me if I wanted one, saying I didn't feel the need!

P . . . . . N . . . . . was basically bored, I found out. Film offers would pour in almost every day, but he could afford to work when *he* felt like it, so turned most of them down. What he didn't turn down was the chance to play practical jokes. I'd heard that once at a party given by M . . . . . J . . . . . at Virginia Water, just outside London, N . . . . . had hired some film extras and dressed them in police uniforms. At the height of the party, when nearly everyone was half-naked and smoking pot, the extras burst in blowing whistles and yelling it was a police raid.

Most of the best-known faces on British television and in the pop world were there. Panic broke out, especially when someone rushed in with a camera and flash. I was told the poor 'photographer' was almost killed: his camera was smashed and he ended up in hospital. When everyone finally calmed down, N . . . . . stood up and said, 'That had you scared shitless, didn't it?' and collapsed on the floor, laughing hysterically. No one else saw the joke. But he was a big spender, and generous with favours like film parts, and so stayed popular on the social scene.

One afternoon he phoned me and invited me to a party he was giving to celebrate the signing of a new movie part.

'Wear your sexiest clothes,' he said. 'It's going to be a really sophisticated night. I've got them all coming.'

I chose a new French creation by Dior I'd bought only that morning in Harrods. It was made of dark green shantung silk and cost a fortune. It offset my complexion and, at the time, my dyed black hair.

N . . . . . said I looked ravishing when he picked me up. And I did.

As we sat in the back of the Rolls on the way to the Inn on the Park, where the party was being held, he started to laugh. I asked what was so funny.

'Just had an idea, Rochelle,' he said through his laughter. 'Let's say you're my sister tonight. That'll surprise them all. You might even get a movie part!' he roared.

I still couldn't see what was *so* funny, but agreed, as it was an amusing idea, at least.

'What about my accent?' I asked.

'No trouble, no trouble,' he laughed. 'I did come from those parts. *And* I ran away from home, if you remember.'

I didn't, but then I'd given up reading fan magazines when I was sixteen.

The guest list for the party read like a *Who's Who* of the film, pop and stage world. N . . . . . spent about an hour going round with me, introducing me as his long-lost sister. Everyone was fascinated. But when he added that he was 'thinking of having some good old-fashioned family entertainment with me later,' the joke fell a bit flat. The first time he said it I smiled politely and shrugged. By the thirtieth time, I didn't think it at all funny. And neither did anyone else.

N . . . . . had disappeared to talk to three young starlets who stood listening to his boring jokes and stories with their eyes and mouths wide open. I circulated among the guests, keeping up the pretence of being his sister, and making up all sorts of stories about our young lives together. The champagne was flowing, and everyone was relaxing and seemed to be enjoying themselves.

I felt a tug at my elbow. N . . . . . was pulling at me, a serious look on his face.

'Have you seen F . . . . . S . . . . . ? I heard he's just arrived. Straight from California. Spoke to him yesterday. I've gotta see him. Do you know where he is?'

I shook my head.

'No one's mentioned it to me,' I said 'Are you sure he's here?'

'Positive. They phoned from reception,' he said, looking around him. 'Stand on this chair and have a look-see,' he suggested, lifting me up.

I looked around but there was no sign of F . . . . . S . . . . .
A few guests turned to see what was happening. Suddenly,
without realizing what was happening, I felt the front of
my dress being ripped off. I was so shocked I couldn't move.
I wasn't wearing a bra, and immediately put my hands in
front of me.

'See, folks?' N . . . . . shouted, a broad grin on his face. 'My
sister keeps it out in front too. A family tradition!' he laughed.

Everyone in the room was staring at me. Some laughed
nervously. I tried to get off the chair, but he pushed me back,
pulling my arms down from my breasts.

'How's about letting the guys kiss what God provided for
the use of mankind?' he laughed brutally, trying to put one
hand up my skirt.

I hit him across the face. He let me go and I rushed
across the room, tears pouring down my face. The guests
moved aside silently. The only sound came from the hi-fi
system where a Rolling Stones record was playing.

I grabbed my coat and caught a taxi home, crying all the
way.

I'll never know why he did what he did, or what he got
out of it. I never saw him again, and he made no attempts to
get in touch with me. The following morning, however, an
envelope containing $500 was delivered to me, and a scrap of
paper with his signature on it. I told the cab driver who had
brought it to wait. With a pair of kitchen scissors I cut the
money in half, wrote his name on the front of the envelope,
resealed it, and sent it back. I wouldn't even have used that
money for charity.

It was the Hath situation all over again, only worse. At
least with Hath it had been private. But in front of all those
people, those famous people! That decided me. I'd had
enough of the jet-setters and the 'glittering' world of show
business.

As far as I was concerned entertainers were the clowns
of a capitalist society, the court jesters of the Establishment.
What was it a Roman Emperor once said? Give the people
circuses and you'll be able to control them. Oh, how right
he was! Movies, pop music and television were the new

146

opiates of the masses. Surrogates for the people, as Cohn-Bendit put it, I think. New means to control the working classes, that's all.

After my humiliation I would concentrate on what I knew I was best at – sex. At least I knew where I stood – or lay.

I started to attend aggro meetings once a week again . . .

But ideals, even the most determined ones, do not keep body and soul together. I went through my book crossing off the names of the jet-setters I had been mixing with. I was left with eight names! Hardly enough for a girl of my tastes and standards. Roger was kind, and took me out a few times, but I didn't want to lean on him. I was trying to be independent, after all!

I talked my situation over with Meg Thomas, probably my closest friend. Meg was, and still is, as far as I know, the only call-girl I've met with a B.A. from a very prestigious university. She was a super girl and we'd hit it off from the minute we met in the Canary Club. Meg had come to London to teach in a primary school – and actually did for a while.

She was living with her boy-friend Nigel, another teacher, in West Hampstead. According to Meg, Nigel was a happy-go-lucky sort of chap, who enjoyed his rugby and pints of beer. Not like his friend Leslie, who was a tough, go-ahead, ambitious man with big ideas. Or so she thought. Leslie was a rep for a champagne company. Nigel began to talk about marriage, houses and kids – the last thing Meg wanted. So she split from him and moved in with Leslie, in Kilburn. He began taking her on his rounds, visiting night-clubs and restaurants – the sort of places that bought the champers for £3 a bottle and sold it for £30. Through Leslie, she got to know the London night-club scene fairly well. Hostesses and managers would sit and chat with her as she became recognized. Well, typical male that Leslie was, he got jealous!

They had a blazing row one night, in which he said she was bad for his business, and he was fed up with her tagging along. He beat her up – pretty badly, from what Meg tells me – and she had to stay away from school for two weeks.

Leslie, frightened that Meg would go to the police, quit his job and left London.

Meg saw her chance – the cunning so-and-so! – and being tired of snotty-nosed brats she asked the wine company if *she* could get orders for champagne, as she now knew the London scene. But that didn't last long, especially when she found out that some of the girls in the clubs were earning more in one night than she did in a month. So she started working as a hostess in one of the clubs, before going independent and getting on the conference circuit.

You see how easy it is!

I kept in touch with Meg, and was to use her later on in my other work. And at the time of my experience with N . . . . . , she was an absolute darling.

'What you need,' she said, 'is organization. I know one of the leading madams in London. I'll fix up an introduction.'

She was as good as her word. I met Julia the following week. I'd heard of her, of course. There were only two or three madams operating rings of girls in London worth knowing. Julia was one of them.

We met in that marvellous tea-shop in South Audley Street, the one with the expensive but beautiful cakes. Julia had said she would be carrying a copy of the latest *Vogue*, but at first I thought I'd approached the wrong person. There was this delightful little granny figure, sitting with *Vogue*, carefully picking at a cholocate gateau with a fork. She had grey hair, shortly cropped, with a small velvet hat sitting primly at the back of her head. A Harris Tweed two-piece suit (mid-calf length, I remember), 'sensible' shoes and a matching handbag completed the picture. No wonder I thought I'd made a mistake!

She was European, I never found out where from, and had a lilt to her voice. We introduced ourselves, and only after she had insisted on pouring some tea for me and ordering a cake did she lean forward, her grey-blue eyes twinkling and her thin lips smiling sweetly, and start speaking in a low voice about what I'd come along for.

'I've heard of you, dear,' she said. 'As a matter of fact I'm a little annoyed. You've taken one of my best clients.'

I ran through my short list in my mind, but had no idea who she was talking about.

'No, I'm not going to tell you,' she went on. 'All I'll say is that it's someone who enjoys S and M and bondage.'

That covered six of my eight!

'Now to business,' she said, still in the same soft voice, the smile on her face. 'Meg tells me you would like to join my ring.'

I nodded.

'I think it's time I put my life on a proper footing,' I smiled.

'It's a good idea,' she said. 'I hear your specialities are whipping and bondage. Is that so?'

'I keep my clients happy,' I replied.

'Good. Now what do you know about my ring of girls?'

'Nothing.'

'We deal only with the top people,' she told me. 'There are about twenty girls altogether. We've got Government officials, two MPs and international figures.' She paused, watching a blue-rinsed lady trying to decide which cakes to buy. 'Yes,' she sighed. 'I think I've built up the ring carefully. My number is known to the top madams in Rome, Paris, New York, Tokyo, Toronto and Berlin. And I've got their numbers. So if any of my clients are going abroad, I can give them a number. We must make sure our men are always satisfied,' she chuckled.

I laughed.

'The customer is *nearly* always right,' I said. 'But how does the ring operate?'

'Simple. The clients get in touch with me first. Then I call you to let you know when to expect them. You don't even know who they are until they appear. They give you the money and you bring my percentage once a week to my flat in St. John's Wood.'

'How much is that?'

'Oh, it varies. You charge £30 for an afternoon. I get £5. Dinner dates are £50 up to five hours and I get £10. You keep all the gifts like watches and so on. I'm not greedy,' she smiled.

She then asked me about my flat – was it in a good area, did I have enough equipment, did I need any more clothes and so on.

She reached for her handbag and took out a small pad and wrote a number on it. Tearing the sheet off, she passed it over to me.

'My number,' she said, 'in case you get into trouble or want to chat. Otherwise I'll call you. I have your number, Meg gave it to me.'

'You mean I'm working for you now?'

'Was there any doubt? I like you and think we should get on well together. Oh, another thing,' she said, lifting her hand in the air. 'Change your number and let me know what it is as soon as possible. We don't want your old clients annoying you, do we?'

I shook my head. I was still trying to take in the fact that I was now a member of an exclusive call-girl ring. Julia stood up, and leaned over and kissed me lightly on the cheek.

'Welcome to the ring,' she said and wandered off, pausing at the counter to pay and gaze with smiling eyes at the range of cakes. Just like any lady in her sixties, wondering what to buy her grandchildren . . .

My clients varied from the straightforward lonely to the downright bizarre. I found it fascinating that the top men in business, industry or politics are among the loneliest men I've met. They would pay between £50 and £100 just to sit and have dinner with me and talk about their general interests in life. You see, I put no pressure on them, made no demands, which their professions and wives always did. Some of them wanted me to tell them fantasies, and I must say I even amazed myself with my inventiveness! I told all sorts of erotic tales from one about the woman who could only achieve orgasm in the back of a Rolls-Royce and became a chauffeuse to the story about the man who kept six women chained in his basement. It was not up to me to work out the reasons why clients wanted this sort of thing. I never asked. But they kept coming back.

But most of them were sexual deviants, with one kink or

another. Some of them were amusing, in a sort of way, but others were really dangerous, in my opinion.

One day Julia phoned and told me to meet a Mr Gray at the Hilton. We had lunch, and afterwards he invited me up to his suite. Once inside, I asked him what business he was in. Torture, he said, smiling. He was in his mid-forties, very strongly built and had large hands. I laughed. Oh no, he said, he wasn't joking and his speciality was cutting people up. To prove his point, he pulled out a flick-knife, saying it was only when he saw the blood flowing from the cuts he made that he could have an erection.

I was terrified, but tried not to show it. I talked and talked, not stopping for a minute. Half an hour later, I managed to get away. Julia went crazy. She struck him off the list and blazed at me for going into his suite in the first place. 'Always have them come to you,' she told me. She could have saved her breath – I'd learnt the hard way.

I think the easiest money I ever earned when with Julia was when I was paid £150 to sit in Fortnum & Mason's tea room at a table on my own without any panties on. The client sat at a table against the wall watching me. I stayed for an hour and then left. Outside, in Piccadilly, he gave me an envelope with the money!

The most common request was for whipping. I did this nude, or with only stockings and suspenders, or sometimes wearing special costumes paid for by the client. One of the men, a member of the House of Lords, always asked me to dress in my panties and stockings before being beaten.

My leather gear was specially made in a little shop off Regent Street. To the passer-by it looked like an ordinary clothes shop, with leather jackets, belts and trousers in the window. But inside, behind the main showroom was another room with rows of bizarre clothes waiting to be collected.

The client would usually draw me a sketch of what he wanted, and the shop-owner never batted an eyelid as he pored over the drawing, working out the best way to make it.

Some of the designs asked for by clients would have killed me had I worn them. One man wanted me encased in leather from head to toe, with only an opening at the crutch. When

I pointed out to him I couldn't breathe he compromised. I could wear a leather hood with holes.

Julia treated all her girls like daughters. If we fell ill, she sent us to a private clinic and footed half the bill. We all had to visit a private doctor twice a week to check for venereal diseases, and a copy of the doctor's report was sent to Julia. She had a complete up-to-date filing system on the girls and clients, with cross-references about likes and dislikes.

Each girl had her own set of ethics. I refused, for example, to indulge in anal sex. I'd tried it during my agency days, and did not like it at all. I wasn't that keen on oral sex, but did it to clients as long as I washed them first. And as the soaping and rubbing – I used a face-cloth shaped like a mitten – turned the men on, none objected. And later, when I visited a few brothels on the Continent I found the girls always insisted on washing clients before *any* form of sex. What's that saying about cleanliness is next to Godliness?

As far as the clients were concerned, Julia's set-up was perfect from their point of view. Only she knew their true identity and if I was taken out to dinner to a small club or they came to my flat they always used a false name.

And clients would do almost anything to try and keep the secret. One man, who introduced himself as Mr McNab, and who only visited me in the afternoon, would put on this phony Scottish accent, thinking I would be fooled! But I never once let him know I knew it was false, but would sigh and talk about 'the old country'.

And then clients often arrived without enough cash on them. And somehow, they always felt guilty about leaving without paying the correct amount. So I would have a Mr 'John Toogood', asking me if a cheque made out to cash would suit me. 'Of course,' I would say, and watch them sign a cheque with a completely different name. I would say nothing and keep up the pretence.

It was so, so easy to discover the real identity of a client if I wanted. My greatest source was newspapers, especially *The Times* and the *Daily Telegraph*. Most of them ended up there at some point, a photograph or description sparking off my memory. Sometimes I would be taken to favourite restaurants of the clients where the head waiter would call them by their true name. The client usually took the head waiter aside and had a whispered conversation, while I stood waiting. 'Just making sure we get a good table, my dear,' I would be told when the John came back. And for the rest of the night, the client would be called by the name he had given me! The tips, I remember, were usually very large on these occasions.

One thing I did notice about false names, however – which later Viktor was to compliment me on – was, whenever a man thought of a different name, the new name would have either one, or both, initials of his real name. For example, if a man was called Tom Smith, he would tend to change it to Terry Saunders.

Exposing them never entered my mind. I was still going out to my meetings every week, dressing up in old clothes and even putting a wig on, so as not to be recognized either by clients I might bump into or by my revolutionary friends when I was working. But I felt the same about my clients as I did about jet-setters. Knowing little snippets about their sex lives was not going to start a revolution.

And anyway, I was beginning to realize that my leftist colleagues could not really *do* anything with any information I may have picked up. My clients were Establishment. And very powerful. What chance did a bunch of young passionate kids have against them? None. If I ever did find out something, I would work out a way of using it for the cause on my own. And in such a way that it would not end my career.

The chance came sooner than I expected.

One day, a tall, craggy-looking man in his fifties appeared at my door. He walked with a slight stoop and had silver-grey hair. I recognized the walk, the face and his manner of speaking. He had been on television and radio more times than I could remember. It was Sir John Aylmer-Theobold, a high-ranking Civil Servant. He introduced himself as 'Jack Alexander'!

He began to visit me once a week, and we had a nice, easy relationship. He seemed very insecure for a man in his position and enjoyed being humiliated by me. Once or twice he asked for another girl, whom Julia supplied, and while I stood over him dressed in a leather corset and holding a whip, the other girl would urinate on him.

His beatings were followed by intercourse as a rule, except when there was another girl involved. These sessions would normally only last a few minutes, but seemed to satisfy him.

One afternoon we were lying on my bed, when old Theobold started talking about himself and the pressures of his job. I was half-listening, nodding sympathetically and saying, 'Of course, darling,' and 'Certainly, my love,' every few minutes, watching the clock to make sure he did not outstay his time.

And then I suddenly realized what he was saying! The old fool was rambling on about his Ministry, what changes he was about to make and how the new people he was putting in would mean a change of policy. 'Because we tell the Minister what to do, you realize,' he said. I nodded, not really following everything he said, but enough to know that surely what he was telling me was classified information!

After he had gone, I did some hard thinking. It would be silly trying to blackmail him directly. I would be finished on the call-girl circuit in London. Julia would see to that. And anyway, the money I could get from Theobold would be nothing compared to what I would be paid by someone who really needed the information.

And as I said, as far as my revolutionary friends were concerned, what would they do with it?

There was only one thing I could do, I thought. Take my information to a foreign intelligence service. That way I could kill two birds with one stone. I would be paid, and paid well. And by getting Theobold the sack, I would be helping the revolutionary forces. At last!

The next day I worked out the practical side of my idea. For a start, I scrapped the idea of making sure Theobold got the push from his job. To do that I would have to go to British Intelligence – wherever *they* were, as I had no idea then. If

I did that then Julia's good relationship with the Foreign Office and various Ministries would be finished. And so would I.

I didn't fancy going to the Russians. Being a Marxist/Leninist, I believed in an alternative society based on Mao's China. And the few Russians I'd met had not impressed me.

I'd heard the CIA paid fortunes for *any* kind of information. They loved any hint of a scandal involving upper-crust Englishmen, especially Government figures. Hadn't the Americans pulled out every bit of sexual muck in the Burgess — McLean and Philby affairs? So the CIA was the obvious choice.

The American Embassy in Grosvenor Square certainly gave the impression of being able to pay well. White marble, huge golden eagles outside the main entrance and a lavish interior convinced me I was right.

It was autumn, and I wore a short skirt and woollen jumper with a fur coat. I didn't want to look as if I needed the money, after all.

At the desk I asked a bored-looking girl if I could see the 'Head of Intelligence.' She told me to take a seat, after taking my name. Three-quarters of an hour later I was still waiting. And becoming very, very angry! Finally I was called.

'Someone will see you now, Miss Duvalle,' she said. 'Take the lift to the second floor and you'll be met.'

A young girl who looked no more than eighteen, and wearing jeans and a university windcheater, was waiting for me.

'Miss Duvalle?' she asked.

I nodded.

'Follow me, please,' she said.

We walked along a long corridor, passing offices on either side.

'You do realize, don't you, I want to speak to the head of security. The CIA, which no doubt you've heard of.'

'Sure, sure,' she said, without turning. 'The CIA.'

I was fuming. And when I was shown into a small room

with a desk, two easy chairs, a filing cabinet and a picture of President Nixon on the wall, I thought that was the last straw.

The girl showed me in and left, closing the door behind her. Behind the desk sat a young man who looked as if he'd just left college.

'Hi,' he smiled, showing a row of perfect teeth. 'I'm Chuck Dawson.'

I glared at him. Surely he couldn't have anything to do with the CIA?

'Are you connected with American Intelligence?' I snapped.

He reached into his pocket, and pulled out a packet of Pall Mall cigarettes, took one out and lit it.

'Please sit down, Miss Duvalle,' he said, blowing smoke in my direction. I sat down in one of the easy chairs, however. Which meant I was looking up at him. 'Now, what is it you want to tell us?'

I shook my head.

'I'm telling *you* nothing. I want the Head of the CIA.'

He puffed on his cigarette.

'Of course,' he said. 'I'll report your visit to the proper authorities. But only after you give me the facts.'

I wanted to leave. I told him yet again I would only speak to the Head of Intelligence.

He leaned forward on his elbows. He was wearing a black blazer and an open-neck shirt under which I saw a gold cross hanging from a chain.

'Now listen, Miss Duvalle,' he said quietly. 'The fact that you're in this office at all means you've made your mind up to tell us something. Now how in Heaven's name can I help *you* get through to the correct authorities, if you don't help me?'

I thought it over for a few seconds, and then nodded. I opened my coat and crossed my legs. His eyes darted hungrily to my thighs. I'll get back at you one day, I thought. And I did – but more of that later.

I had decided not to tell them the information was coming

from me. I wasn't sure about their connection with British Intelligence, and I might land myself in trouble.

'I've got this friend,' I started, 'who's a call-girl. I'm not, in case you were wondering. I'm a computer programmer,' I said quickly. 'Now supposing I *was* a call-girl, however, and managed to get some information from a high-ranking client, would you be able to use it, and how would you repay me?'

He was beginning to look interested. But not that interested. He seemed to be more concerned with the tops of my legs than what I was saying.

'Very interesting,' he said. 'Why do you think your friend wants to pass this stuff on to us?'

'She doesn't agree with the way the country's being run.'

'Fair enough, fair enough,' he said, stubbing his cigarette out. 'Do you know if she's seen anyone else about it? Talked to other people apart from you?'

'Oh, no. I'm the only one who knows. I'm sure of that.'

'Well, as I say, I'll make my recommendations,' he said, sighing as if bored with the whole thing. 'Can you give me any idea what she's found out?'

I wasn't going to tell him everything, so gave him broad hints. He pulled out a notepad and scribbled some of the details down.

'Well, thank you very much, Miss Duvalle,' he said when I'd finished. 'Now if you'll tell me how to spell your name, give me your address and phone number, I won't keep you any longer,' he smiled, his pen poised over the pad.

I uncrossed my legs and sat back in the chair, parting my knees as I did. I heard him catch his breath as he caught sight of the flesh between my stocking tops and panties.

'I'd like to talk about this in more *comfortable* surroundings,' I said, opening my eyes wide.

'Why . . . yes, of course. But first I must make sure it's worth following up. Talk . . . to . . .'

'Oh it will be,' I said, smiling at him.

'Yes . . . ah . . . I'm sure,' he stuttered. 'Now details please, Miss Duvalle.'

'Call me Rochelle, Chuck. All my *friends* do. When will we

meet to talk further?' I asked.

'I'm a very busy man. Why not call me in a couple of weeks?'

'Of course, Chuck,' I smiled, allowing my legs to open a little more.

He actually blushed, and quickly lit another cigarette. I told him what he wanted to know and left. As I walked along the street, I was shaking with fury. He hadn't even mentioned money! And not so much as a thank you! Imperialist swine, I thought. I was glad I hadn't told him the whole story. I would find someone who disliked capitalism as much as I did, and *then* give the full story.

I caught a cab to the Russian Embassy in Kensington Palace Gardens.

But it was just as bad, if not worse, there. The place was not quite so grand as the Americans'. A dark-haired woman with black spectacles and her hair drawn back sat at the reception.

'I'd like to speak to the Embassy's Chief of Intelligence, please,' I asked her.

'In connection with what matter?'

'Personal.'

'Certainly. Please be seated.'

A few minutes later a young man asked me to follow him. At least they didn't waste time here, I thought. They take these things seriously. He stopped in front of a door which looked as if it could do with repainting, opened it, and waved me in. The walls were pale green, there was a small worn carpet on the floor in front of an old, battered desk, over which a large globe hung, and a couple of imitation leather chairs for typists to the side of the desk. There were no windows in the room, and behind the desk a poster of Leonid Brezhnev had been *taped* to the wall.

'I must be in the wrong place,' I said to a small squat man who sat behind the desk, wearing a dark suit. His hair was short and black and combed straight back. 'I want to speak to the Chief of Intelligence.'

'I know,' he said, and nodded at my escort who left. 'Please sit down,' he added, waving at the typists' chairs. I perched on one and he asked me the same sort of questions I'd had at

he American Embassy. I tried about six times to discover
who *he* was, but he ignored me each time. I didn't even find
out his name!

'Now what is this information your friend has?' he finally
asked, poking his little finger into his right ear and twisting
about.

I gave a little more detail than I had to the Americans.
While I was speaking, the Russian put his feet on the desk,
yawned widely a few times, and picked his nose, while staring
at the ceiling. He even pulled out a comb and ran it through
his hair!

When I had finished, he sniffed deeply, took his feet off
the desk, stood up, walked across to the door, opened it and
looked around at me.

'If you turn left you will be back at reception. Goodbye.'

It took a few seconds for his words to sink in. He hadn't
shown the slightest interest in what I was saying. And their
manners were worse than I'd seen at the American Embassy.
And as far as money was concerned, he also had not mentioned it, even when I put it to him bluntly that 'my friend'
would want payment.

I felt a fool, and almost cried with rage in the cab on my
way back home. So much for superpowers. I didn't know
what to do, where to go with my information. It was all so
hopeless. How could *anyone* change a system when no-one
was interested?

Two weeks later I phoned Chuck Dawson at the American
Embassy and reminded him of his promise. I would have one
last try, and then forget the whole thing. I suggested we met
at Mirabelle's, 'as it's not *too* expensive', I said.

To my surprise, he actually turned up. I had dressed to kill.
My silk, figure-hugging dress was low-cut and I wore a simple
velvet choker round my neck. My hair, still dyed black, was
shoulder length, and I'd spent nearly an hour over my make-
up, putting on light green eye shadow, a smooth base for my
skin and just a touch of rouge. I wore dark red lipstick. He
was stunned.

I let him buy a couple of bottles of champagne with
dinner, which I insisted on paying half for, telling him I

knew he 'didn't get paid much in that job of his'.

We returned to my flat, where I used every trick I knew i
the book. He climaxed three times that night – 'a record
he told me later, and said I'd given him the best sexu
experience of his life.

'Now do you take me seriously?' I asked. 'Do you believ
me about my friend's information?'

He nodded.

'Of course,' he said, lying back in my bed, practicall
exhausted. 'But as I said before, I reported your visit t
the proper authorities. It's up to . . .'

'Oh, forget it,' I sighed and turned round to sleep.

As far as I was concerned, foreign espionage services coul
get hold of their information somewhere else.

And so I worked with Julia, beating and whipping m
clients, making a lot of money which ended up in Swiss ban
accounts. I went along to aggro meetings every Wednesday
but wondered deep down what good it was doing.

And then about a year after my visits to the Embassies, tw
men dressed like undertakers arrived at my flat . . .

PART TWO

All in the Game

On the 24th September, 1971, the British Government publicly expelled 105 KGB and GRU* agents. The Soviets had been engaged in espionage operations to subvert politicians, with the object of neutralizing British cities and towns. With irrefutable evidence of this plan, the British Government acted ruthlessly. So ruthlessly in fact, that Leonid Brezhnev and KGB Chairman Yuri Andropov held an emergency meeting at Moscow Airport. (Brezhnev had to break off a tour of Eastern Europe.)

The implications of their meeting were twofold. First, it meant a complete withdrawal of the KGB's key saboteurs and assassins, part of the secret Department V, from Europe. For British Intelligence held Oleg Adolfovich Lyalin, a member of Department V, and the Politburo believed he was about to disclose the identity of the best-trained and most ruthless of the KGB operators abroad. Across the whole of Europe Department V personnel disappeared, showing a terrifyingly extensive network prepared to use violence if necessary to cripple peacetime Governments.

Secondly, and this had more long-term implications, Soviet Intelligence strategy was altered. Instead of openly subverting key figures, the KGB began to engage more in what Lenin had called *ruf morde*, or character assassination, resulting in the destruction of confidence in a nation's leaders.

This had long been in line with Soviet Intelligence thinking. When the KGB plan the destruction of a country in political terms, it thinks less of their own strengths than of our weaknesses. Should there be a war with Britain, for example,

* The GRU is the Chief Intelligence Directorate of the Soviet General Staff. Theoretically it is separate from the KGB, but as John Barron indicates in his book *KGB* (Hodder and Stoughton, 1974) it would appear that the GRU is a military subsidiary of the KGB, whose members normally occupy a large percentage of Embassy posts.

it is not so much Russian military power that the Soviets will count on as the possibility that Communist-inspired unions and specially trained espionage groups will close the ports, stop the trains, attack centralized electricity plants, halt the mines and generally cripple the civilian infrastructure on which military movement must depend.

In August 1971, *Paris-Match* published an interview with Jan Sejna, a Czech defector to the West, in which Sejna claimed that he knew of plans 'to sabotage the London subway system in the event of serious political difficulties'. Communist agents would then organize demonstrations and accuse the British Government of 'deliberately halting the underground to prevent public protests'.

Ruf Morde then becomes the psychological equivalent of the physical neutralization of a country.

These objects of paralysing Britain's civilian network and the exposure of total corruption of the British economic and political leadership is a policy which is the constant aim of the KGB.

After the expulsion, however, the strategy for achieving these objectives changed. The Soviets have become more subtle in their attempts to infiltrate the civilian infrastructure and are using the STB, expert in the war of dirty tricks. The growth of union strength and disillusionment with British policy abroad, especially over Vietnam and Rhodesia, had created a suitable climate for this new strategy which had been decided on before September 1971.

The Profumo affair, although not a Soviet ploy in the first case but later used as such when the KGB planted an agent on Profumo, added more fuel.

The war of the spooks took on a new dimension. The underworld, the world of spies and informers, saboteurs and assassins, was filled with recruits, many of whom did not know the ultimate aim of the people they were working for.

Sandra Brown, alias Rochelle Duvalle, was one such recruit . . .

CHAPTER 11

I woke up one night in January 1973 with a feeling of panic. I was on my own in the flat and my body seemed to be gripped by a huge vice. I couldn't move, and lay staring at the ceiling. My mind was racing and sleep was impossible. I was thinking of the Red Circle.

To all appearances, it was complete. But I suddenly became aware of the *scale* of the Circle. We had covered almost every area of possible entrapment. And that's what worried me! Perhaps it was *too* big. I'd been so busy building up the network over the past nine months, I hadn't stood back to take an objective look at it. Of course, that was Mikhail's job but as I've said before, when it came to matters of the underworld, Mikhail and his bosses were fairly naïve.

The network was only as good as its back-up services. One loophole could destroy the whole plan. Before the Big Kill took place, I had to strengthen the shadow supports. We were so near the final drops I became over-worried, as Mikhail said. But from that night in January until the middle of March when the Big Kill took place, I lived on my nerves. I tried not to show it, of course, and after speaking to Mikhail once about it, I never mentioned my feelings to him again.

But with George, I checked out all the pimps, pushers, brothel-owners, property-owners who rented flats to prostitutes and the girls themselves who were all working indirectly for us, to make sure there were no weak links in the chain. There were none.

There was one area that caused me more headaches than any other – the drug scene. Mikhail had pointed out to me at the beginning of the build-up that the normal entry for the STB (and other intelligence services) into vice rackets was through narcotics.

'Drugs are a sort of blanket over other vices like prostitution,' he said. I agreed. I'd seen far too many girls killing themselves on drugs, normally supplied by the vice ring they worked for.

What the STB did was 'eliminate' the narcotic dealers, and replace them with their own people. Up until I started on the Red Circle, I'd had no dealings with the drug racketeers. They were ruthless and would kill if they felt their territories were being threatened. Which means there is a constant war between the 'straight' drug controllers and intelligence services who try to break into the market.

It was up to me to stop this war, and arrange a truce.

I managed it in these last few months before the Big Kill, but quite simply, I couldn't trust the controllers. With millions of pounds at stake, why should they keep their word to us? So again, you can see why I was worried.

The truce was arranged at the end of January. Watson, Viktor, and a Dutchman I'll call Van Klees who controlled most of London's narcotics, his two bodyguards and myself, met in the office of La Plume D'or late one night. In the club were a dozen of our own muscle-men. I didn't like it at all. This was serious organized crime, and I was not into that, believe me. It had taken me months to trace Van Klees and then persuade him to come across and fix up the meeting. Viktor represented the 'other' dealer who wanted to hit the London scene. There had been two deaths among the Dutchman's dealers, both organized by the STB. One of our own pushers had been beaten up so badly he would not be able to walk again. Something had to be done.

I'd never met anyone like Van Klees in my life, and I don't want to again. He was small, wore gold-rimmed glasses, and dressed fastidiously. He didn't smoke or drink, but sat through the meeting sipping a glass of lemon tea. His face was round and smooth, his brown hair parted neatly on the left. Had I bumped into him at a party, I would have taken him for an accountant.

He would have seemed an honest, trustworthy man, had it not been for his eyes. Steel-grey in colour, they stared through me and were not quite fully open. Everything I said, as I discovered later, he remembered. He was like a machine with no normal human emotions. Not once did I see him laugh. He spoke about the deaths of his dealers as if he had lost a book of stamps. Life meant nothing to him. When not talking business, as I found out later over a meal, he tended to say nothing, his eyes moving slowly around the room the whole time. He was the most frightening character I'd come across in my work for the Circle.

Our deal was simple. We had no intention of taking over the London drug scene. We had our own sources for drugs in Eastern Europe, but nothing compared to the Dutchman's worldwide network. We were prepared to buy supplies from him, as long as he let us do our own pushing.

'Why?' was all he asked, when we'd outlined our proposition to him.

'I'm in the prostitution racket, Mr Van Klees,' I smiled, doing some quick thinking. 'A lot of my girls get ideas about going off on their own, or exposing my network. If I can have my own pushers providing them with drugs, then I'm safe.'

He looked straight at me. No one moved. The internal phone rang but Viktor picked it up and quickly put it down again.

'Okay,' the Dutchman finally said. 'Give me your requirements and I'll see they're met. You do know the cost, of course?' he asked.

I nodded. It was extortionate, but we had no choice.

We all knew that it was only a truce. Van Klees would see the chance of breaking into the prostitution racket himself and get rid of our pushers. And then it would be all-out war. But if we could hold him off for two months, we couldn't care less. Luckily, we were able to do just that . . .

There was another reason why I insisted on keeping the net as tight as possible. Our first operation carried out during September – December 1972 made me wary. And taught me a lot about feathermucking.

As I've said, the catalogue was growing. In under a year we'd spotted an MP in a Charing Cross bookshop loading himself up with books on homosexuality; we had photographs of another MP in one of our controlled brothels being dressed in woman's clothes; we had a third MP in the catalogues who had attended a wife-swapping party using a false name and accompanied by a prostitute he claimed to be his wife. He had answered an ad. in a contact magazine, naturally not knowing that every person who responded to *any* ads in most of the contact magazines, had his or her name forwarded to us. We had about four peers on cine film being 'disciplined' by 'English governesses' in flats around central London.

Given my background I'd expected *some* kinkiness among the ruling classes, but what was coming in from the Circle staggered even me!

Not all of the possible targets could be used. Some of the MPs were only backbenchers, and the worst that would happen to them would be expulsion from their party and perhaps a divorce. A target had to fit certain qualifications, according to Mikhail. We found such a target in August 1972, and began to work on the drop.

He was a well-known columnist for a right-wing newspaper. He had everything going for him, as far as we were concerned. He was influential through his regular newspaper column, and was a great favourite with the rich and famous, being asked to all types of parties and functions. He owned two homes – one in Highgate and the other in Buckinghamshire – where he often entertained VIPs, especially politicians, leading industrialists and Trade Union leaders, many of whom were on our list. We'd heard that he enjoyed group sex but perhaps most important of all we knew he would collect 'interesting people' for evenings of 'stimulating discussion'.

Harmless enough, you may think. But once he'd been persuaded by us to have a couple of orgies, and we then exposed the fact, it would be easy to suggest that *all* his 'stimulating evenings' were orgies. And think of the names which could be dragged in at that point!

He'd been spotted in the first place by a bookseller called Herby, in Soho, who'd seen him on television a few nights before. The target was concentrating on magazines and books which contained explicit group sex. Working on this, the bookseller said he would soon be stocking up on some really hot stuff and would save some for 'the gentleman' if he wished. All the Circle's booksellers had been coached personally by me to make this approach and, as the mark usually tended to say 'No, thanks', at first, were trained to draw the mark into the conversation during which they would admit their weaknesses, if not directly, then by implication.

The mark turned up a week later asking about the hot stuff.

Herby shook his head.

'It's been a bad week, sir,' he said. 'The police've gone crazy. Everything's tightening up. We were raided last week – just the day after you were in – and the good stuff's gone.'

The mark would turn to leave, but Herby would lower his voice (as instructed in their training with me) and say it was still possible to get special goods to customers.

'How's that?' the mark asked.

'We do it hush-hush, sir. Give me your name and address and I'll have it posted to you. No, sir, I don't want your *real* name and address, but don't you have a pick-up address or something like that? An accommodation address?'

And so the mark moved on to the next part of the network! In this case, he was back within three days, with an accommodation address picked out of a national newspaper. In other words, one we had already penetrated and knew as soon as he registered.

Of course, all the play-acting about accommodation addresses was completely unnecessary as Herby had recognized him from the start. Which was why Mikhail didn't put the mark on even light surveillance – for once a mark has a private address, he soon begins to see its possibilities as being wider than for merely getting a few dirty books through the post.

We began slipping in type-written invitations to take part in swingers' parties for 'the discreet'. He ignored the first few, but eventually sent off his £10, or whatever, and said he wanted further details. Which we gave him. We rented a flat for the night, and I had two of my girls seduce him, in a bedroom which had been furnished with cameras. When I

got the pictures back, it was easy to see he'd done this sor
of thing before!

After that, we got him involved in more and more group
sex scenes. What we wanted, of course, was a party in hi
place, either in the country or London, when we would make
sure a few 'newspaper photographers' would burst in behind
'the police' to 'upgrade' the whole operation. That's when I
would come in, and promise him that nothing would happen.
He'd be grateful and we'd keep him in the can until later.

Well, when the time did come for him to be host, you can
imagine our shock when he took four men and three girls
down, not to his fine country mansion, but to a glorified
bed-sit in Brighton!

Mikhail later told me this was a textbook case in every
respect except one. We had the wrong man! Our mark wasn't
the well-known columnist after all. True, he looked like him,
but we should have carried out surveillance on him, when we
would have seen him going to his dreary clerking job in the
City each day, instead of Fleet Street.

(*This story was, and still is, a source of mirth to the CIA, who
often cite it as 'a classic case of how* not *to spy'. It contains,
however, the main ingredients of a successful feathermucking
operation* – ARR)

What it taught me was that if things are going *too* smoothly,
then check and double-check the mark. And if there are any
suspicions about his identity, or his being a plant from the
other side, forget it.

I didn't even take any chances with Lord Kingwood when
I began working on him. But I'll come to that soon. Something else happened in between which almost made me give
up the whole operation . . .

Just before Christmas 1972, I went to a party given by Lord
Mansewood in his flat in Sloane Square. There were quite a
few people I knew, including Julia, whom I had not seen for
over a year since setting up my own ring of girls. We were still
friendly, chatting often on the phone, and she bore me no
grudges, even though I'd taken a few of her clients with me.
As I'd discovered, there were enough fish in the sea for a

dozen madams to operate successfully.

Julia wanted to know if Lord Mansewood was one of my clients. I laughed, shaking my head. What she, or anyone else did not know, was that Mansewood was in fact my sugar daddy, and had been for years. He'd taken me under his wing during my jet-set days, but had no idea what I did for a living. As far as he was concerned I was a computer programmer, my usual cover story. The STB wanted me to drop him, but I refused. Apart from anything else, we'd never had sex. Once, I went on a long week-end to Paris with him, but we had separate bedrooms and went sight-seeing only.

'Jimmy', as I called him, was the chairman of a nationalized industry board and it seemed to be his mission in life to introduce me to eligible young bachelors with a view to marriage. He could never understand why I always broke the relationship off, the poor old dear!

That night he had someone else lined up, a man I hadn't seen before, but read about in the newspapers – Richard Bailey, the industrialist and merchant banker. He was also a leading socialist, whose donations to Trade Union pension funds and the Labour Party were well-known. I respected him from what I'd heard. He came from a poor, working-class background in Newcastle, had struggled to the top on his own and, at thirty-four years of age, seemed destined to become a Member of Parliament.

He was about five feet ten, had dark wavy, almost curly hair, and a rugged, strong face which was always lightly tanned. He wasn't loud in any way. His clothes were neat and almost old-fashioned; he didn't insist on telling you the latest story about so-and-so, and at the party he stood most of the time in a corner watching everyone else. But when I spoke to him I had this amazing impression of strength behind the façade. A sense of presence.

Mansewood left both of us together. We discussed this and that and finally I asked him about his work for the Labour Party.

He chuckled.

'Yes, people always ask me that,' he said quietly. 'I suppose you think I'm a hypocrite owning all these factories and two houses and driving around in a Rolls-Royce?'

'No, certainly not,' I said. 'We all do what we feel is right at the time,' I added, thinking of my own situation. 'But out of interest, how *do* you reconcile the two?'

'It's not easy,' he laughed. 'But seriously, and without wanting to bore you, I was born into a very poor family. I saw the way politicians used poverty and the working classes for their own ends, promising the moon for a vote. Of course, once elected they did damn all in effect.' He paused and nodded at an acquaintance.

'Go on,' I said, a bit rudely.

'I'm sure you don't want to hear my political views,' he smiled.

'Oh, but I do. Believe me,' I told him, and he could tell from my tone I was serious.

'Seeing the politicians were as corrupt as the petty crooks I knew as a kid, I swore to myself that if I ever found myself in a position to positively help the working classes in my own way, then I would do it, and to hell with politics. And believe me,' he said, his eyes looking directly into mine, 'I think I've done more good for widows, pensioners and the poor than a lot of Socialist politicians.' He laughed. 'But we're getting heavy. Let's change the subject.'

I can't remember what we talked about after that. My mind was literally spinning at what he'd said. Surely he was doing the same thing as I was? Helping the people in a positive manner. I was staggered. I was by his side all night and as I left with him to go on to dinner at Brown's Hotel, I saw Lord Mansewood wink at me. I shook my head.

But, as it turned out, my sugar daddy was right in this case. Richard and I began to see a lot of each other. I looked forward to my nights and occasional lunches with him. We were like children, laughing at the most ridiculous of things, enjoying just going for walks in the park, or sneaking into a movie in the afternoon where we would sit and hold hands like two teenagers. We went to discos like Tramp and Annabelle's and danced until we were almost thrown out.

And on the nights when I couldn't see him, when I was

with one of my clients, or working for the Circle, I was filled with a sadness, a desperation to stop what I was doing, and rush off and see him.

In other words, I was in love with the man.

Oh, yes, I knew I was breaking all the rules of the game. I knew what had happened to Norma Levy when she fell in love with Colin Levy and how he ruined her career by threatening to expose Lambton to the Sunday newspapers. Call-girls or, as I called myself at the time, courtesans, do not fall in love. They can't afford to, it's as simple as that. And yet there I was, madly, hopelessly in love with Richard Bailey.

Suddenly I had a meaning to my life. Richard, who never found out what I did, and I would sit for hours talking about politics. Really nothing else! Of course we had sex, but it was natural, beautiful, and seemed so right. There was no question we would not be good lovers. We didn't even discuss it. On my second date with him, after a meal in a Swiss restaurant in Belgravia, we went to his flat off Regent's Park, had a few drinks and began to make love. And he never made demands. We knew instinctively what the other wanted and did it.

And then I became foolish. I let some of my work with the Circle slip. I delegated more to George, used one of the swallows to go out with marks instead of me. I thought Mikhail was going to kill me when he met me at the Bayswater safe-house not long after.

'What the fucking hell do you think you're playing at?' he screamed at me, when I entered the lounge. It was the first time I'd heard him swear, and I felt frightened.

'What do you mean?' I said, sounding insulted.

'Don't play games with me, Sandra,' he fumed, his face white with anger. 'You've been running around with that Bailey character! Letting our work suffer!'

'In what way has it suffered?' I wanted to know, feeling defensive.

'You know you are the only one who can deal with certain marks. And yet you let swallows take them out. Why?'

'They haven't ruined things as far as I know,' I said, smiling, and taking a cigarette out, went to light it.

Mikhail slapped the cigarette from my hand, sending my lighter flying across the room.

'You'll stop seeing him, do you hear? And from today,' he shouted. 'He could be from the other side as far as you know.'

'Well, that's up to you to find out, not me,' I said angrily

Mikhail glared at me for a few moments and then grabbed my shoulders. Shaking me furiously he yelled into my face.

'Do you realize the work that's gone into this operation? The money? The time? Do you really think you could have managed this on your own? Don't forget, it's us who put your naïve ideas of socialism and communism into practice. *You* would still be selling your body for a few pounds each night!'

I pushed his hands off me and stood up.

'Don't worry!' I screamed. 'Your operation'll go ahead. And succeed. And when it's finished I don't want to ever see you again. I'm going to get married. You hear? Married!' I lied. 'In fact we might even get married *before* the Big Kill, if we feel like it,' I yelled, knowing instinctively I should not have exaggerated my lie.

Mikhail did not say anything but looked at me through half-closed eyes, a twisted smile on his face.

'Nothing will stop the operation now,' he said in a flat, quiet voice. 'I'll see to it personally. Goodbye, Sandra. I'll be in touch.'

That night I could hardly sleep. I felt like telling Richard the whole story and running away with him. But that was useless. I wasn't running from a small gang of thieves in the East End of London. I was involved with a world-wide organization. I decided to go through with the Big Kill, as I'd told Mikhail, and then give the whole thing up. I may have exaggerated about *when* I was going to marry Richard. But I knew I would – and so did he. We *had* discussed it the night before.

The following day we'd arranged to meet in Richard's flat. This we did fairly often, as his office was near the flat, and it gave us what he called 'necessary privacy'. I had the key and let myself in shortly before midday to prepare a light lunch for us. I enjoyed these home lunches. Again, they were normal.

I went straight into the kitchen and began pottering about, humming in tune with some music on the radio. It was only when I was putting the cheese soufflé in the oven that I realized something was wrong.

Richard always left his breakfast dishes on the kitchen table. Three times a week, a cleaning lady would come in – on Mondays, Wednesdays and Thursdays. She would put the dishes in the dishwasher and generally tidy up. As Richard, like most bachelors, tended to eat out in the evening, the kitchen always tended to be tidy.

But it was Tuesday. There were no dishes on the table. Had he stayed out all night and forgotten to tell me? Feeling jealous, more than anything else, I went through to the bedroom to see if his bed had been slept in. I stopped at the door, my legs weak. I stared in horror at the floor beside the bed. There, lying in his pyjamas, his hands stretched towards me, his face in the carpet, was Richard. He was dead.

Strangely enough, I didn't cry. I sat down on a chair in the bedroom and looked at him. I sat there for maybe an hour – I don't know – and then calmly walked back to the kitchen and telephoned Mikhail.

'Richard's dead,' I said.

Mikhail didn't say anything for a few seconds.

'How do you know?' he finally asked. No hint of feeling for me.

'I'm in his flat. I found him.'

'Get out!' he snapped. 'And if you've touched anything wipe it. We don't want the police to start questioning you.'

'How do you know the police will be involved?'

'They always are, aren't they,' he said irritably. 'I presume it's not natural causes, is it?'

'I don't know,' I replied, feeling as if the whole thing was a nightmare, and it wasn't me who was speaking.

I did what Mikhail had instructed and left carrying the soufflé in a plastic bag, which I dumped in a waste-paper basket in Regent Street.

I can't remember much about the next week. I had no energy, no will left. I lay in bed, not eating, not going out, not answering the telephone.

Two things preyed on my mind. One was when the newspapers were delivered two days later. Richard's picture and the story of his death were on the front pages of every paper. They also gave the cause of death. A heart attack, it was discovered after a post-mortem.

And secondly, I remembered something about the bedroom when I found Richard. There was a slight, acid smell in the air which had gone by the time I left his flat. And with a feeling of total nausea which left me too weak to move, something Viktor had told me months before came back.

A favourite method of Department V of the KGB for carrying out 'wet work' was by the use of prussic acid. I remembered Viktor proudly telling me how it was done. A glass phial was placed in a narrow tube about eight inches long, he had said. A spring in the tube set off a small charge which crushed the glass, spraying the poison out as a vapour. When the acid was inhaled, the blood vessels contracted, just as in a heart attack. Once dead, however, the blood vessels relaxed, and any examination of the body would show a cardiac arrest. Viktor had pointed out that the agent doing the wet work took an antidote tablet before and after carrying out his mission.

I knew what the smell was now. And I knew the STB had killed Richard . . .

I wanted to get out. To be finished with the lot of them. I told Mikhail and he laughed.

'It's far too late for any feelings of conscience,' he said. 'We told you right from the start what you were doing. You've enjoyed the material benefits, haven't you?' he grinned. 'And please don't get us wrong, we appreciate your wonderful organizational abilities.' Smiling, he lowered his voice, speaking softly. 'Look, Sandra, the Big Kill's only two months away. After that, you're a free agent. You can go anywhere in the world with the money you've made and we'll be giving to you. And you'll be safe. We don't forget our riends and you're part of a very powerful organization, on't forget.'

What he said made sense. But I could never forgive them or what they did to Richard. Never. Mikhail, as usual, eemed to know what I was thinking.

'I know you're upset about Richard Bailey,' he said, ropping the smile. 'But please don't think we had anything o do with it. I'm sorry I flew off the handle the other day. thought our whole operation was going to be ruined. But ven we don't go to such lengths. What . . .'

'Forget it, please,' I interrupted, feeling sick at his hypo-risy. 'We've got work to do. Where's the final list?'

He sighed and put his arm around me. We were in the ayswater safe-house again. 'That's better,' he mumbled, ulling out a sheet of paper from his pocket. There were velve names on it. At the head was Lord Kingwood, ollowed by the names of four MPs, five peers and two leading usinessmen. I stared at it, nodding.

'That seems fine,' I managed to smile. 'There should be o problem getting them along for the Kill. It's only King-'ood who's giving headaches. But I'll get him, don't worry.'

Back at my flat I broke down. I was trapped once more – nd saw no way out. I didn't know who to turn to or what to o. I began wondering what the point of it all was. The Big ill – who was it going to help? I had seen or heard nothing bout organized marches, revolutionary students or workers om Mikhail.

I had been told about the massive disinformation campaign lready prepared which would swing into motion after the ig Kill. But then, I asked myself, what good would *that* do? he British public have short memories. What happened fter the Profumo affair to *basically* alter the way the country vas run? And the Lambton affair? Nothing. What I was doing, vhat I had done, by building the Red Circle was only another nove in the game of intelligence. Scoring points, hoping one ay to win the game. Knowing deep down the world of pooks and dirty tricks had a momentum of its own, which as nothing to do with the feelings of the people who really vant change.

177

The end result is sometimes a Vietnam, a Chile. But nothing really changes. The people are still downtrodden no matter what Government rules them. The 1968 'revolution' in Paris, when the workers and students united for a few days, was crushed by the police controlled by the capitalists. In Hungary they used tanks and slaughtered God knows how many in the name of freedom. It's all the same. A game. The people are the pawns.

Oh, yes, I was bitter. I still am. I was tired of it all. Tired of spending a lifetime following hazy ideas, tired of politics - tired of everything, in other words.

And I had to stop the Big Kill before it was too late. But there was no way. The Circle was too tight, the final plans drawn up. I had to follow it through. Or be killed. So you see, I had no choice. I was trapped.

Of the four MPs involved, I had personally brought two of them into the Circle, after they had been spotted in the net. One was the wife-swapper who enjoyed group sex. What made it worse, as far as he was concerned, was that he was a Catholic. (We had spotted another Catholic MP with a young woman who turned out to be his secretary and with whom he was having an affair. But he was small fish, so we dropped him.) The other attended a call-girl regularly in Maida Vale and had a Lolita complex. I set about upgrading both drops in the same way.

To meet each MP, we worked out his area of contact first. This included everything from his hobbies and, in this case, his weekly constituency meetings. A circle was drawn and all the information on the mark written round it. A dot in the middle was the principal agent, or the person who would make the introductions. I drew a circle with my interests or area of contact round another dot, representing me. The idea was to find someone who knew us both, or whose area of contact overlapped the target and myself.

In the case of the MPs it was fairly simple. With all the peers we knew, it was only a question of arranging a party for the introduction to be made. But I assure you, you can get to meet literally anyone with this method it's so foolproof.

I was always introduced as the owner of La Plume d'Or. The reaction was always the same.

'My goodness,' the mark would comment. 'We didn't think night-clubs were run by beautiful young ladies like you.'

'Well, I was left some money by an aunt and thought I'd have a bash at it,' I'd say modestly.

They were immediately fascinated, and we would discuss the problems of running a night-club. I would offer them an honorary membership, asking if they would like it sent to the House of Commons or their private address. Most of them gave their private address.

A couple of weeks later I would drop a note, reminding them who I was, and inviting them to pop into the club for drinks. Nothing ever happened at the first meeting, except I would make sure they came down while the place was fairly empty, in case they were worried about being seen. Once they were satisfied, I began to upgrade in earnest.

I would invite them to a 'private party' in the club, or have someone known to them and working for us, like Mallette for example, invite them down. The camera and monitors would be in position and we would get a few incriminating pictures, the girls going into their normal poses. We would store these pictures for future use.

Then we would have another party, at which a fight would break out, and the 'police' – i.e. our muscle-men kitted out in uniforms – would arrive. But just before the police came, we would hustle the targets out. And, of course, were they grateful!

It was a question of getting them to trust us, and the fake fights – really tough, with blood being spilt – helped to do just that. Soon our marks were attending parties regularly, being filmed, and entered into the album, the book which would be finally released to Press and other MPs after the Big Kill.

And naturally, at all the parties, from the first one on, we would provide all facilities – girls, drink and, as the parties moved out to the Mansion, bedrooms.

Sounds easy, doesn't it? But staging these parties took up most of my time, and sometimes a target would never appear after his first visit to the club. The sort of men we

were after were no fools. They knew what they had to lose
We only concentrated on the targets on whom we could pi
something specific and work on that area. I mean, an un
married MP would not mind very much if he was seen a
cocktail parties with beautiful women or attending week-en
gatherings in a country house with a different woman eac
time. That's *Private Eye* stuff, and not in our league.

Another MP in the net was a retro-operation. He'd had
homosexual affair years ago and we knew he was still payin
the other man to keep it quiet. We simply took over the rol
of the other man, who was a greedy hustler anyway, an
threatened exposure. That *was* simple.

The fourth MP on the final list was interesting. He had n
personal sexual deviations. He only enjoyed watching blu
movies. Now there's nothing wrong in that, but when w
discovered he had put his signature to a private motion i
the House to ban private movie clubs, we had him. Th
hypocrisy ratio again. He had been spotted going into a clu
in Berwick Street, on the pretence he was 'investigating it fo
his upcoming speech'. And when we had a private film shov
with Dutch and German blue movies at the club, we filme
the whole thing making sure a couple of our girls were i
the picture.

It had been slow, but then upgrading any target takes tim
With Kingwood, things moved a little faster, but I was sti
careful. Looking back, I think it must be the best piece o
feathermucking ever to get on the books.

'Well, what do you think of him, then?' Mikhail aske
smiling thinly. After Richard's death, and as the Big Ki
approached, our relationship was becoming cooler. I put
down to two things: Mikhail knew I suspected the STB o
murdering Richard, and he was obviously nervous. If th
Big Kill did not come off for any reason, then he, along wit
about a dozen others on the London station, would go th
way of Granny and Simenovsky.

'Oh, he's charming, darling,' I answered. 'An absolut
dear. And he seems to like me, which makes it easier.'

We were in the office of the massage parlour.

'When did you last see him?' Mikhail asked.

'Two nights ago. We went to Churchill's.'

'Churchill's? That's hardly the sort of place lords frequent, is it?'

'Exactly,' I said. 'That's what makes sure we'll be able to drop him. It was my suggestion, and as he'd never been, thought he'd give it a try.'

'Was he recognized?'

'I don't think so. The place was practically empty when we were there. But I had Ivanov come along with a camera and flash, and photograph us sitting in a booth, saying it was for a West German magazine.'

'Good, good,' Mikhail grinned.

'Of course I created merry hell. You should have seen me! I called the manager, whom we're already paying as you know, and said unless we were given the film Lord Kingwood and I would sue the restaurant for invasion of privacy. Poor old Ivanov. He was hustled back between two waiters and made to open his camera and take out the film, which I then unwound. Oh, and by the way,' I said, going into my handbag and pulling out an envelope, 'here are the pictures. From the camera Ivanov shoved in his pocket.'

Mikhail laughed mirthlessly.

'Ah, he's a good man, Ivanov. I'll see he gets rewarded for this,' he said, spreading half a dozen glossy prints out on the desk. 'Excellent. What now?'

I sighed.

'Well, I don't want to rush things. You've had a twenty-four-hour surveillance put on him?' Mikhail nodded. 'Any irregularities?' 'None,' Mikhail said. 'Telephone tapped?' 'Of course,' Mikhail nodded. 'Normal calls. Phones his wife twice a day from the office.' 'Anything from his office monitor?' 'Nothing. He's clean.' 'That's what they all say,' I said sarcastically. 'Remember the first case? I'd rather be sure this time. Did you manage to get his bedroom and front room monitored at his flat?'

'Simple,' Mikhail said, clasping his hands together. 'The old telephone company trick. His maid let us in. There are no irregularities there either.'

I shook my head.

'I don't believe everything I see or hear now, thanks to your training,' I said. Mikhail half-closed his eyes, staring at me. 'I'd still like someone there in the house.'

'A charlady started this morning.'

'Good. How did you plant her?'

'Well, you know the English, my dear,' Mikhail smiled, stretching his arms. 'They've got to have their staff. And nowadays who wants to work as a domestic? Kingwood's maid was doubling as a cleaning lady, so we sent our woman along with forged references saying she'd been recommended to him, and did he need any help? That was ten days ago.'

'And they say an Englishman's home is his castle!' I laughed.

It still amazes me how easy it is for a foreign power, or even big business espionage networks, to invade someone's privacy. If the charlady trick had not worked, we had another card up our sleeves – naturally! We would have staged a robbery either at his house or office. The police – or rather, my 'friends' in the police – would have advised Kingwood to have a police plant around for a while, as the robbery could have been an inside job. So poor old Jimmy would end up with another secretary or maid. And we would have inside surveillance.

'So when are you seeing him next?' Mikhail asked.

'I'm not sure. Let's keep him under surveillance for another week. He's too big for us to take any chances.'

Mikhail agreed and stood up, holding his hand out.

'Take care, Sandra,' he said as I shook his hand, 'I'll leave Kingwood to you and be in touch in a week.'

Jimmy Kingwood looked at me over his half-lens glasses, his grey eyes twinkling in the candlelight.

'So what else do you do in this club of yours apart from eating and dancing?' he asked.

'Oh, Jimmy! What are you implying?' I teased. 'This is a properly run club. And I'm very proud of it.'

It was Jimmy's first visit to the club. About ten days had passed since I'd seen Mikhail, who'd phoned the previous day to say all the surveillance reports were negative.

'Right, I'll start the upgrading,' I told him, and phoned Jimmy at his office and reminded him of his promise to come to my club sometime.

I'd been out with him three times before, not counting our introduction. The principal agent I'd used was a literary agent, one of the fringe people. You find them in every city – advertising men, public relations people, artists, publishers and so on. They hang around the famous and wealthy, and having the strange idea that they're smooth and cosmopolitan tend to mix with foreigners. The fringe is only useful sometimes, as most of the people who make it up are so amateur in almost everything they do, they can be an embarrassment, rather than a help. They all like the idea of working for a foreign power, but would probably ruin any operation they were involved in.

But they have their uses. I knew this girl was friendly with Kingwood, and said I would pay for a party in her flat in Chelsea, if she could arrange to have Jimmy along.

'I've got this super idea for a project,' I told her. 'But I can't tell you now. It's all hush-hush.'

Like most of the fringe, the chance of having a free party with a bit of intrigue thrown in, was too much for her to resist. I met Jimmy one week later.

He was not quite what I expected. From what I'd seen of him on television, and read in the newspapers, I had the impression of a stuffy, boring, dry-as-dust member of the Establishment. In fact, he turned out to have quite a sense of humour, even if it was sometimes levelled at himself.

The poor man had been in for a lot of lampooning and satirizing from political writers and cartoonists. He was sitting on two commissions concerned with public morals, being the chairman of one. When he became a lord, Jimmy involved himself in the more general aspects of politics like public morals, prison reform and abortion laws.

He was honest, sincere and dedicated to his work in these fields. He was also one of the biggest fish the STB, or any other foreign agency, had netted.

At the party we chatted generally.

'Don't you find the House of Lords pretty ineffective afte the Commons?' I asked him.

'Well, we still have *some* influence, you know,' he said 'And it does give one time to follow one's own beliefs instead of being caught up in the race for votes.'

I nodded.

'You mean like your commissions on public morals?'

'Exactly. But then I'm getting a little tired of being called a Crusader against Sin, as if I was the first and only one to speak out against corruption. Old Gladstone was doing it in the nineteenth century, for goodness' sake!'

I steered the subject on to general politics, and I could see he was impressed by my knowledge. As I said before, I made it a point to keep up with what was going on. And my weekly meetings in Islington kept me informed about the other side.

'What do you do for a living, my dear?' he finally asked.

'I own a little night-club in central London. But not the sort your commission would be interested in,' I added quickly, laughing. 'It's more a sort of supper-club, if you know what I mean.'

'Sounds fascinating. I must visit it sometime after the theatre, if that's all right with you?'

'Of course. I'll try and be there myself.'

'And how did you get into this strange business of night-clubs? Was it luck or otherwise?' he smiled.

I lowered my eyes.

'I'm afraid it's neither. You see, Lord Kingwood, I'm divorced,' I said quietly. 'Over something quite silly. But my husband left me and luckily my aunt had a bit of spare money and suggested I should do something with it. So I opened my little club.' I sighed. 'But it's hard work.'

'I think that's wonderful,' he said. 'So many women would have gone to pieces in your situation. Yes, I'll definitely come down and visit you.'

I gave him the club's card and he handed me his business card.

He had bitten . . .

I called him up a week later. He remembered me immediately.

'Rochelle, my dear! How are you? How's the club business?'

'Fine,' I said. 'It couldn't be better, in fact. It seems as if people enjoy going to a supper-club instead of the other sorts of clubs.'

He said gruffly, 'Too many rip off places around.'

'I should think so, too,' I added. 'I'll tell you why I phoned, Lord Kingwood . . .'

'Jimmy, please.'

'Thank you, Jimmy. I was wondering if perhaps we could have lunch. I've got something I'd like to ask you.'

'Charmed, my dear. Absolutely charmed. I'm rather busy, however. Let me look at the diary,' he said. 'Would next Tuesday suit you?' he asked a few seconds later.

'Perfect. Where?'

'Unfortunately, my club is gentlemen only, and the food is marvellous. But that's out, so how about . . . how about that marvellous Russian restaurant in Horseferry Road. It's near enough to the House, where I'm speaking in the afternoon.'

'Perfect,' I said. 'See you there at one.'

It was a good choice from my point of view. The Old Russia restaurant is often used by MPs and peers, being within walking distance of the Houses of Parliament. In fact, it even has a division bell connected to the House of Commons, in case an MP has to return for an important vote. It's been decorated in pre-Revolution style and has three separate areas. And the food! It really was marvellous, from the huge tray of *hors d'oeuvres* right through to the little sweet cake for dessert.

We had a bottle of Russian champagne with the meal and Sambouki with the coffee. Kingwood was a wonderful table companion. He kept me amused with stories of MPs and his days on the bench all through lunch.

I was wearing a pale blue trouser suit, a high-necked white jumper, and very little make-up. My hair had been cut short and I'd had the black dye rinsed out, so I was my natural

auburn. Jimmy hadn't recognized me at first, but I could se
he approved of my new look. Which, of course, was why I'
decided to change.

Over coffee, he asked me what I had wanted to see hir
about.

I pretended to be nervous, turning the small coffee cu]
round and round in its saucer.

'Well, Jimmy, the club's making a lot of money now, to b
honest,' I said, looking down at my cup. 'And I've got enough
to keep me going. I was wondering . . .'

'If you should invest?' he interrupted.

I looked up at him. Both arms were on the table, and hi
tall, craggy figure was hunched forward. His balding head
his tiny glasses and prominent, square jaw made me pictur
him as the famous judge he once was.

'No, Jimmy, I don't want to invest. I want to give it to
charity.'

'You want to give it to charity, my dear?' he said slowly
as if cross-examining in court. 'How much?'

'Half my profits,' I said, my face straight, and widening
my eyes a little, to give me that little girl look everyone said
I had.

'Are you serious? I mean, I think that's one of the most
amazing and kind things I've heard in years. But you know
the old saying about charity beginning at home and all
that?'

'Yes, yes,' I sighed. 'But I really have enough. And then
there's my aunt I mentioned. She's going to leave me everything in her will. And it's enough for me on my own.'

'Your own? Surely you'll get married again?'

'I doubt it. I had . . . I had a very bad experience with my
husband. I don't really trust many men now,' I said, almost
whispering, forcing a lump to my throat as if about to cry.

'Don't speak about it if you don't want to,' Jimmy said,
laying his hand on my wrist. 'Another time, perhaps.'

I sniffed.

'Thank you, Jimmy. So what charities should I put my
money in?'

'Oh, there are hundreds to choose from,' he said. 'Oxfam,

Help the Aged, Cancer Relief, Dr Barnardo's Homes, Prison Reform . . .'

'Isn't that what you're involved in? Prison Reform?'

'Why, yes, I am. When I can find time, that is.'

'Well, I happen to think it's long overdue. I'll give my money to them. If you give me the address I'll send something off this afternoon.'

He laughed and pulled out his notebook and gave me an address for the Howard Penal Reform League. We finished our coffee and parted outside the restaurant. I *did* send a few hundred pounds off – anonymously – that afternoon.

We met for lunch twice after that, once at the Ritz and the other time at the Dorchester. I always turned up wearing a trouser suit and jumper. Never once did we as much as kiss each other goodbye in public. That would have ruined plans.

And then we met in the club. For Kingwood's visit, I'd told my regular hostesses to bring in their boy-friends, for a night on the house. The part-timers were told not to report. I asked all the girls who were coming along to wear something respectable. Meg, who was normally on reception, was specifically told to come along.

Jimmy and I shared a bottle of white wine. I asked how his work was going, what he had been doing, and so on.

'Do you like the club?' I finally asked, when he made his remark about other things going on.

'I'm very impressed, Rochelle. Very impressed. But how do you manage on your own?'

'I do have some help, you know. A few of my friends come down some evenings. But,' I said softly, 'it's not the same as having a man run the place.'

Jimmy coughed nervously.

'You mean your husband?' he asked.

I nodded.

'Look,' he said leaning forward, 'I know you don't like talking about it. But are you sure he won't come back if you ask him?'

'There's no chance. Not after what I did. Oh, it was so, so silly!'

'Would you like to tell me about it now? I had some experience with broken marriages in my barrister days.'

I leaned on the table and ran my fingers through my hair.

'It's . . . it's so painful,' I stammered, fighting back the tears. 'It only happened last year. I had an affair,' I said quickly and looked up at him, blinked and bit my lower lip.

'Is that all?' Jimmy said, surprised. 'My goodness, that happens all the time.'

'Between women?' I asked quietly, still staring at him.

I saw him stiffen. His eyes widened in amazement.

'*What*? You? You mean . . . you had an affair with another woman?'

I nodded slightly.

'It was nothing, really. I enjoyed it, I'm not denying that. But I don't know why I did it. I just don't know.' I covered my face with my hands and began to cry.

'Now, now, my dear,' in that famous soft voice of his. 'It's all right. These things happen. I can understand it, don't worry.'

'Oh, it's terrible, Jimmy. What am I going to do? I went to a psychiatrist after my husband left me. He said the same as you. It was all right. I'm what is known as bisexual, you see. I enjoy men and women. Oh, I shouldn't be telling you this,' I said and rushed away from the table, dabbing at my eyes as I did.

I stayed in my office for five minutes. Tidying myself, I returned to Jimmy, who was still at the table.

'I'm sorry, Jimmy,' I said, sitting down opposite him. 'It's not fair of me to tell you things like that. Apart from the psychiatrist, you're the only person I've told.'

'I appreciate it, my dear. And the secret won't go further, believe me. But tell me, have you finished with this other woman?'

'Yes and no,' I said, hesitating. 'She's actually in the club tonight. She works for me now. But we don't . . . we don't . . .'

'You don't have to say it,' he said sympathetically. 'I know what you mean.'

We were silent for the next few minutes. I saw Jimmy glance around the club a few times, obviously wondering who my 'girl friend' was.

'Would you . . . would you like to meet her?' I asked. 'As you know all about me now, I don't mind.'

'If you think that'll help, by all means.'

'I feel better already for having told someone else,' I smiled. 'I'll just introduce her as my friend, all right?'

He smiled and nodded.

I brought Meg over from reception and the three of us sat for about an hour drinking wine, until Jimmy said he would have to go.

I saw him to the door.

'She's a charming girl, your friend,' he said as we stood outside, waiting for a cab. 'And sensible. I'm sure if you spoke to her, you could end the thing once and for all.'

The cab had drawn up as he spoke. I opened the door for him.

'Ah, but that's it, Jimmy,' I said as he brushed past me. 'I don't know if I want it to finish.'

The cab drove off, with Jimmy's face staring at me out of the back window.

The next stage was obvious. Believing that I had taken him into my confidence, I would hold a small party in my flat. Meg, two lesbians, a few men from the club and some girls would attend. Meg and I would hold hands and whisper to each other through the evening, laughing and chuckling like teenage lovers. The cameras would be set up, of course, and some preliminary photographs would be taken for the 'album'.

Jimmy, you see, had first been spotted by the network several months previously in a Soho porn shop with some other members of the commission. It was a bona fide raid, and even before our plant gave us the news, the story of the visit had hit the evening newspapers. But what the newspapers did *not* say was that Lord Kingwood was seen browsing among the section of lesbian books, a few of which he took away with him.

Still we had nothing. All the members of the raiding party, followed immediately by the police, had taken some books as 'evidence before the commission', as the newspapers said. I was only later through police contacts in the vice squad, that something more positive came to light. Kingwood would often visit the vice squad after their raids into porn shops. Before the magazines and books were destroyed, he would insist on going through them, and would *always take away some lesbian books.*

This was our lead, and why I used the pretence I did. And also why he was such a big fish. If we could slide him into a sexual situation, where he was either watching, or taking part (touching, stroking, giving directions) in a lesbian scene, with a group of other people, then the exposure would definitely rock the British Establishment.

There was only one flaw. A man in Kingwood's position could always say he was 'investigating the sub-strata of pornography for his public inquiry into morals'. Like every well-known man, he must have considered what would happen if he got into trouble, and arranged some safeguards or 'outs'. My problem was to get him into a situation where he had no outs.

I played on sympathy. There I was, a poor, confused girl who'd fallen into a trap of lesbianism, lost my husband through it, and desperately wanted to make something of my life. He already felt sorry for me. After the party he would try and do everything he could to get me back on the straight and narrow. Which would be difficult – I would make sure of that.

The party went according to plan, although I was furious when the two genuine lesbians disappeared into my bedroom to make love. That could have scared him off for ever. But I managed to get Jimmy out of the house without his knowing what was going on a few feet away from him.

The next morning Jimmy was on the phone.

'I think I'd better have a word with you, my dear,' he said, seriously.

'Yes,' I said in a small voice, grinning from ear to ear. 'When?'

'Tomorrow, lunch. At the Inn on the Park. One o'clock,' he ordered, and hung up.

Perfect! he was beginning to talk to me like an angry husband.

I turned up just after one. He was waiting in the bar, drinking tomato juice. He didn't waste time with small talk.

'I think you're mixing with the wrong type of people,' he said, glaring over his spectacles. 'That party last night was not the sort of thing you should be attending.'

I stood, my head down, pouting like a little girl, while he rabbited on about responsibilities and it was time I grew up, and so on. I kept nodding my head.

'But I don't have anyone to turn to,' I finally said. 'You're the first person that's shown any *real* interest in me.'

'What about your parents? Where are they?'

'Dead. I was brought up by my aunt,' I lied.

He was silent. We went through for lunch, but he was not in the mood for eating.

'New friends, that's what you need,' he said when coffee came. 'I'm going to make it my business to make sure you meet them.'

And he did. We went to theatres, cocktail parties, operas, ballets and talks together. There were always other people present, and he rarely took me along with him, but he would meet me. After the show, or whatever, was over, he would leave with a friend. He didn't want people to think he was having an affair with me, or anything like that!

These were the *public* meetings. The private meetings told a different story. They began by my phoning him late one night crying down the phone.

'What's wrong, my dear?' Jimmy said, sounding concerned.

'Oh, I feel terrible,' I wailed. 'You know that nice young man you introduced me to last week – Robert Thorn? Well, we had dinner tonight, and he took me home, and tried to . . . tried to . . . you know,' I cried. 'But it's not that I'm upset about, really. I pushed him out of my flat. I thought it was disgusting! What am I going to do?' I asked, crying. 'I think I'd better go back to the psychiatrist. There *must* be something wrong with me.'

'Nonsense. Absolute nonsense,' Jimmy snapped. 'You get in a cab and come right over here. That young brute — I thought he was a decent sort, as well.'

Over at his place, I cried some more, and then gradually composed myself. He comforted me, like a father comforting a daughter. But I was no child, and he knew it. I was an attractive woman, he had told me so himself.

'You're so helpless, aren't you,' he murmured, as he hugged me gently. 'So helpless.'

That was the beginning. I began to 'depend' on him for everything. Advice, what clothes to wear, what books to read and so on. He loved it. No woman had asked him for this sort of advice for years. He felt manly and important in a way no amount of commissions could make him feel. And eventually one day (or night — I'm not sure which) he brought it out into the open.

'You know, Rochelle, you've become something special to me. I think about you a lot. Worry about you. Wonder what'll happen to you in the future.'

I took his hand between mine.

'I know this may sound silly, Jimmy, what with our age difference and all, and if you don't speak to me again after what I'm going to say, I wouldn't blame you.' I paused. He squeezed my hand. 'I think I love you,' I whispered. 'Not in any sexual way, you understand. Just pure, beautiful love.'

He sat still, his head tilted to one side.

'I know,' he said at last, very quietly. 'I feel the same.'

Our relationship became more intense after that night. He started buying me presents, giving me money and arranging meetings at all times of the day and night.

'I'm going to sell the club,' I said one day at his flat. 'Go abroad and try and start anew.'

He was shocked.

'You can't. I won't let you,' he protested.

'But you've got a career, a wife, and a reputation to think of,' I pointed out. 'I'm still quite young. Let's face it, Jimmy, I love you dearly and deeply, but what does the future hold for me? Or us?'

'I . . . I need you,' he said simply.

I kissed him lightly on the cheek.

'And I love you,' I said. 'I'll think again about leaving. But seriously, what can you offer me?'

'Everything,' he said 'Everything I've got you can share.'

'You mean you'd leave your wife?' I gasped. 'And what about your reputation?'

'They don't matter any more,' he said stiffly.

'And . . . and what about my being . . . my being bisexual?' I whispered.

'I don't mind. You can't help what you are. Maybe in time I'll help you change,' he shrugged.

I left feeling sad and happy at the same time. Sad in a way I'd led him on so far with an ulterior purpose in mind. He was so sincere, the lovely man. And happy that I'd achieved my aim. Now he had no outs. If he became involved in an affair with me, he could not say he was investigating public morals. He would be seen to be such a hypocrite, the repercussions would last for years, not only affecting him, but many others in the so-called 'respectable' Establishment.

Having Jimmy accept me for what I was, made the upgrading simple. I invited him for dinner in my flat one night. He was surprised to find Meg there.

'I thought we'd better all have a talk,' I said by way of explanation.

He nodded, but was obviously nervous and uncomfortable. Especially when Meg insisted on helping me in the kitchen where we deliberately laughed and giggled over the silliest things.

Jimmy was more relaxed over dinner, helped on by a couple of bottles of champagne. Later, as we sat in the lounge drinking coffee and liqueurs, I suggested putting a record on the stereo. Meg, on my instructions, chose a slow, Frank Sinatra mood album and swayed in time to the music as she went back to her seat.

I jumped up, and grabbing Jimmy's hand tried to pull him out of his chair.

'Let's dance,' I said.

'Oh, no, no,' he laughed. 'It's been too many years sin
I indulged in that sort of thing.'

Meg came up behind me.

'I'll dance with you,' she said.

I raised my eyebrows at Jimmy, waiting for his approval
He nodded and smiled.

'Go ahead. I won't be jealous, I promise,' not quit
realizing what he was saying.

Meg and I danced apart for a track of the album. Bu
the following track was slow and romantic. We moved clos
and put our arms around each other, Meg's hands resting on
my bottom. As usual I was wearing a trouser suit, very tigh
and made of silk. You could see the outline of my brie
panties through it. Meg was wearing a skirt, to just above her
knees, and an open blouse.

As we danced, I felt Meg's hands move against me, her
fingers running down the base of my spine and along the
centre of my buttocks. Jimmy hadn't moved, but wa
watching us with a bemused smile.

I pressed close to Meg, feeling her bra-less breasts through
her thin blouse. I almost laughed when I found she really
was excited, and her nipples were hard and erect. But then
Meg actually *is* bisexual.

She began rubbing her hips against me, her eyes closed
and her mouth slightly open. I glanced across at Jimmy
He was perfectly still, but I could see he was becoming
excited.

Suddenly I pulled away and went over to him.

'Oh, my darling, this is *so* unfair,' I whispered. 'You mus
be bored on your own.'

'No, no, please carry on dancing,' he said. 'I don't mind.
As if I thought he did.

Meg and I danced for a few minutes longer, before Meg
saying she was hot, unbuttoned the front of her blouse dow
to her waist. She flung herself against me, and rubbing her
breasts against me, began to moan.

I pushed her away a little and then bent down and kissed
her breasts. I noticed Jimmy's legs moving as he became
more 'comfortable'. Meg's hand was between my legs, and

194

she moved it round, pressing hard against my vulva. I felt myself becoming wet, but apart from that, felt nothing. Lesbianism just wasn't my scene.

When Meg dropped to her knees, and began to kiss me through the tight silk, I decided that was as far as we would go. That night. As I say, entrapment is a slow business, and I didn't want to undo all my work to date.

I went back to Jimmy and sat on his knee. As expected he had an erection. I pretended not to notice, and nibbling his ear, said there was a time when I would have gone the whole way.

'Isn't that a good sign?' I whispered. 'I must be able to control myself better.'

He grunted. I think he was a little disappointed – in fact, I know he was!

So I arranged a couple of surprises to cheer him up. The first was Meg's 'birthday party' down at the club. Jimmy was amazed to find H . . . . . J . . . . . and M . . . . G . . . . . there, the two MPs I've already mentioned. And they were just as surprised to see each other. But as the evening wore on, and the champagne flowed, everyone relaxed. The club was closed to outsiders that night, and when Viktor turned up with a blue movie all the guests were so high, they thought it was a marvellous idea. The cameras whirred as the movie was shown – it was of course a lesbian scene, with three girls and a series of sex aids, if I remember – and we managed to get some good footage for the album. There's nothing like sitting in the dark surrounded by girls stroking and touching you, plying you with drinks, while you watch explicit sex on a screen.

The whole point of the party, of course, was to make Jimmy and the two MPs feel they were not abnormal. As the old song says, 'Everybody's doin' it, doin' it.' and once our targets begin to think this, they'd go to all sorts of parties, with the attitude 'If it's all right for Jimmy, then it's all right for me.'

(I had already found this on the swingers' circuit in London. Mainly professional people, like doctors, dentists, lawyers, regularly attended wife-swapping parties and orgies.

They know each other, of course, but not one will admit having seen the other at a party. If any member of the group breaks the code of silence, the circuit is automatically ended. I personally know three Harley Street doctors who attend such orgies. The swinging circuit in London is larger than most people realize, although now it is being taken over by the pop world.)

We had two more parties in the club, inviting a few more prominent marks to each. By the time Mikhail and I sat down to work out the final details of the Big Kill, all the targets we needed were well and truly hooked.

We had actually planned the Big Kill for April. But something happened to make us push it forward. And make me even more nervous than I already was.

Meg called me one morning at the beginning of February.

'They were in again last night,' she said.

'Two of them?'

'Yes the same men. Did the usual,' she went on. 'Sat at the bar nursing a couple of whiskies all night. Didn't talk to any of the hostesses and left just before midnight.'

'They didn't ask any questions? Who owned the place or anything?'

'Nothing.'

'Thanks,' I sighed and hung up.

I'd asked Meg to call me if the two men ever turned up again. I'd first noticed them one night at the bar. One was small, dapper and had a pleasant face. He was talking to Ingrid, one of our hostesses, and I thought nothing of it. We did get a few straight clients down at the club. He paid his hostess fee and left quite late.

The other man was taller, spoke with a slight American accent, and was a big spender. And yet he never took a girl out of the club. It just didn't make sense, and I had a strange feeling they were not what they claimed they were – businessmen who travelled around Europe.

I never saw them together at any time, and yet I got the impression they knew one another. Don't ask me why it was just one of those feelings. They would come in

ccasionally and it was always the same. The small Englishman would sit at the bar while the American would surround
himself with girls, and buy champagne.

I asked Mikhail to run a check on them, after taking some
clandestine photographs.

'We don't recognize them at all,' Mikhail told me once he'd
had the picutres sent to Moscow to check against known
British and American intelligence agents, 'but that means
nothing.'

'They *could* be ordinary customers, you know,' I said.

Mikhail looked worried.

'So why do they come down to a night-club that's known
to have hostesses, and yet never take a girl home?'

I couldn't answer that. They had been down four times and
never even hinted to one of the girls about after-hours
entertainment.

'We're moving the Big Kill forward,' he said.

'To when?'

'Three weeks.'

I stared at him. The sort of plan we had discussed normally
takes up to six weeks to prepare.

'It's impossible,' I said.

'If we wait longer, there may not be an operation,' he
said coldly.

I nodded. If the men were DI6 or CIA, then we knew they
were on to us. And they would never let us go ahead. Mikhail
and I knew it would be the job of British Intelligence to stop
the operation.

And so the date was fixed. The week-end of March 10th. I
started the preparations.

CHAPTER 12

The Big Kill would take place out at the Mansion at a week end party. Mikhail and I spent a day going over the potentia guest list. Every target on our list was checked, double checked and either scored off or included. We looked at al the pictures in 'the album'. They were back-up photograph which, while embarrassing individual MPs and Jimm Kingwood (who, as the great Crusader against Sin, had th most to lose), would not have the same effect as photograph of them *all* taking part in a group orgy. Britain's leaders politicians and businessmen – the people who ran the country in other words – caught literally with their pants down!

With the campaign lined up by the STB and KGB, it wa bound to cripple the Establishment. Even the feelings I' had after Richard's death, about the whole thing being useles were changed as we worked on the party. I became convince that the Big Kill would be the greatest threat to Britis politics since Oliver Cromwell.

Finally we had about twenty people whom we knew woul turn up for the party. Jimmy would simply do as I said. H was by now hopelessly in love with me, and apart from tha was openly encouraging me in my affair with Meg. At th parties, Meg and I had gone further and further, until the last one in the club, the three of us had disappeared int the 'rest-room' with its bed and Jimmy had watched Me and I strip each other and perform oral sex on one anothe until we reached orgasm.

We padded out the guest list with our own people Watson, George, Viktor, Mikhail, and some known KG members. These last guests were important, because we ha to tie the orgy in with a threat to national security, right fro the word go. Unlike that silly, overblown Profumo affair when the KGB only came in *after* Profumo was exposed, and using Stephen Ward to try and upgrade the whole mess – with disastrous results as far as the KGB was concerned. We did not want to fall into that trap. Some of the girls from my ring were to be brought along to mix with the guests.

I contacted Van Klees and asked him to organize a few girls and a man for a live show to be put on at the party and to have them sent across a week before.

One of London's leading drug dealers was asked along, and he agreed to come, bringing along a supply of marijuana and cocaine.

Mikhail and I went out to the Mansion and tested all the furnishings, making sure the cameras and monitors were operating satisfactorily in all the bedrooms and, most important of all, in the large ballroom where most of the action would take place.

We were still not satisfied. We called in our own operatives and had a dummy run. It took us four days to get everyone briefed as to what they should do, where they should stand, and who should be in the pictures.

Everything was going according to plan. Everyone knew what they had to do over the week-end. There were five days to go. On the Wednesday night, the two men appeared in the club. Mikhail and I laughed when we heard. It was too late for anyone to stop the Big Kill.

On the Thursday morning, we leaked the news of the party to the popular daily and Sunday newspapers – the *Daily Mirror*, the *Sun*, the *People* and the *News of the World*, swearing each to secrecy, promising different exclusives. The leaks went through free-lance journalists, and the papers naturally questioned the story by phoning the Mansion. Our people there gave out just enough information to convince them.

On Thursday afternoon, Mikhail and I drove to the Mansion in the Embassy Mercedes.

The technicians arrived on Friday morning to test the monitors and cameras yet again. There were the usual squabbles and fights which I'd come to expect. I ignored them.

The actual party was timed to take place from Saturday evening through until Sunday lunchtime, according to the invitations we'd had printed – only to prove we were having a party, if nothing else. But we'd pointed out that guests were welcome on Friday night, if it suited them. All our own people, of course, stayed over Friday night, and in fact only a few targets turned up.

Nothing happened on the Friday night apart from giving them dinner and plenty to drink. Waitresses – my own girls and some from the Embassy staff – circulated constantly with trays filled with glasses of champagne. On each tray was a small silver box filled with marijuana cigarettes for those who wanted them. The girls themselves were dressed in typical maids' outfits – short black dresses, white aprons, but wore fish-net tights and black high-heeled shoes.

Around Saturday lunch-time more marks began arriving. Sir Peter Brown was the first, followed by a few more businessmen. None of the politicians had yet appeared and Mikhail was looking tense. But they eventually turned up during the afternoon.

Four MPs were present, from all three parties. Jimmy came along just before six. Mikhail smiled at me as Jimmy walked in. Everyone we needed was now in the Mansion.

Cocktails were served at 7.30, and the guests disappeared to their bedrooms to change. I wore a long, dark blue, silk evening dress with a slit up the left side to about the centre of my thigh. My hair, still short, had been shaped into a page-boy style, and I put on the minimum of make-up. A Cartier watch – a gift from a grateful client – and a diamond choker completed my dress. I looked the picture of elegant innocence.

During cocktails, I stayed close to Jimmy. I knew we were being photographed, not only by our own cameras, but by the few reporters from the newspapers who were attending incognito. Although as far as I was concerned, it was a simple job to pick them out. They carried little leather handbags, becoming popular at the time. Inside were their cameras. It was all very amateur, but then they were not in the espionage business – well, not directly!

The cocktail hour stretched to nearly two hours – deliberately. When dinner was finally served, everyone became pleasantly relaxed. We had smoked salmon followed by *boeuf en cruete* and ending up with fresh strawberries and cream. No man sat beside another. The table placings had been fixed to ensure that each man had a girl on either side of him.

Over the coffee marijuana cigarettes were passed around and soon a sickly-sweet smell filled the dining room. We moved into the ballroom. It was exactly 9.30 pm. At 9.45 the lights went out and a small stage at the end of the room lit up. Three women and a man appeared. The women began dancing to some loud Rolling Stones music, stripping as they did. A chaise-longue with a rug in front of it stood at the back of the stage. When the women were naked, two of them stood to the side, while the third lay on the couch, her legs wide open. One of the other women knelt in front of her and began kissing her vulva. The remaining woman walked to the top of the couch and stood spread-eagled over the head of the girl lying down. Supported by the man, she lowered herself until her vagina was over the mouth of the girl, who began to perform cunnilingus. The man quickly stripped, and standing on the couch placed his erect penis in the mouth of the woman at the top, who was leaning on her elbows on the chaise-longue.

No one in the room moved apart from the 'actors'. The music changed to a slow rock number, and the foursome changed positions, two women lying on the floor while the man and the other woman began to have intercourse. One of the women on the floor reached behind her, underneath the chaise-longue and brought out a large vibrator, with which she started to masturbate, while her 'friend' kissed her breasts.

I was standing beside Jimmy, and put my hand to the front of his trousers. His penis was erect and I could hear him breathing heavily.

At 10.15 the show ended, exactly on time. We moved out to the swimming pool, taking up pre-arranged positions.

Music from extension speakers played by the side of the pool. Joyce, one of the girls from my ring, put her arms round an MP and began dancing, rubbing her body against his.

All this was being photographed, and later, when released it would be made known that Joyce was a well-known call-girl.

I noticed another of the MPs talking to the drug dealer. The MP was smoking a cigarette. Again this was being filmed. The dealer cracked a joke. The MP laughed. When released, the photograph would show him, 'cigarette' in hand, laughing with a known head of a narcotics ring.

A wide-angle lens was being used with special film to include most of the guests, although we had staged things to make sure our main targets were within reasonable distance of each other.

I saw one of the girls, as instructed, with her hand in a grasping motion in front of Sir Peter Brown's trousers, and looking down. Sir Peter was leaning against a wall, looking at her. What was actually happening was she had just told him she had lost an ear-ring after having it in her hand and was looking on the ground for it.

Later, we would take that original photograph and using the same girl, and a man the same size and build of Sir Peter and wearing the same clothes as he was at the party, re-take a new set of photographs. The difference being that in the upgraded pictures 'Sir Peter's' head would be turned away, his penis would be hanging from his trousers, and the girl would be masturbating him. The fact that the girl was a well-known swinger famous for her Chelsea-set parties, made the upgrading perfect.

By 11.00 pm we had all the photographs we needed. Any further pictures would only be used for back-up, like those in our existing album. The final piece of upgrading was due to take place before Jimmy, Meg and I disappeared to a bed-room for *our* final little scene.

Suddenly there was a commotion in the ballroom. We heard shouting and women screaming and glass being smashed. Most of us rushed through to find two men fighting on the floor. A girl stood against the wall screaming hysterically.

Blood was spattered all over the carpet and furniture. Another man lay, his head in a pool of blood, beside a smashed cocktail cabinet.

A few of our muscle-men, dressed in dinner jackets, pulled the men apart. One of them had a carving knife, covered with blood, in his hands, which was prised from him. Viktor knelt by the man on the floor,

He looked up at the pale-faced, horrified guests.

'He's dead,' he said in a quiet, shocked voice.

The girl against the wall began to sob.

'We'd better call the police,' I said.

Panic broke out. The last thing our guests wanted was the police. Viktor stood on a chair.

'Will everyone please return to the dining room, where we will decide what to do,' he shouted above the hub-bub.

We filed through, Jimmy clinging to my arm. I could feel him shaking. I glanced at the other guests. They were just as bad.

In the dining room everyone was shouting and yelling at once. Some wanted to leave immediately, others began making up stories and some just sat, their heads in their hands, staring ahead in disbelief.

At 11.30 pm we heard the wail of police sirens drawing close. No one moved. The police cars stopped outside the Mansion. I began to walk through to the ballroom. A few others followed me, and then gradually everyone headed silently towards the scene of the murder.

The police burst into the ballroom from one end as we walked in through the other. The body was gone. No traces of blood remained. But the smashed cocktail cabinet and the blood-smeared carving knife were still there.

There were policemen everywhere, including some in plain clothes. They began rounding up most of the guests, and loading them into vans. I was becoming confused as this was not in the plan.

A small man, smoking a pipe, and wearing a fawn overcoat, strolled in and looked around, a smile on his face. He looked directly at me for a brief second and then at Lord Kingwood by my side. He showed no recognition, but I knew who he was. Sir K . . . . . S . . . . . , head of British Intelligence.

Had he even nodded at me, Mikhail, who was staring at him in horror, would have known immediately I was a double agent.

I watched as all the STB and KGB operatives were taken out. The 'reporters' – police plants – tore the film out of their cameras. The technicians came out from their hiding places, some nodding at the police and Special Branch men. A tall, lean man with a bronzed tan walked up to us.

'Quite a party,' he said in an American accent. 'Why wasn't I invited?'

I smiled and Jimmy laughed nervously. We watched as the 'dead man' – one of our plants – was led off, the theatrical blood still sticking to his face.

Jimmy took hold of my elbow. I looked up at him.

'You know, Rochelle – or rather, *Sandra* – you really are rather sweet in a way. And it *was* fun. Thank you,' he said and walked out of the ballroom, leaving me staring after him, speechless.

'Surprised?' the American asked.

I nodded dumbly.

'Yes,' he chuckled. 'He's been working for us all along. But you know what it's like in this business. You can't be told everything,' he added, taking my arm and leading me out of the Mansion for the first of my many interrogations by the CIA and DI6.

I had approached the Special Branch in 1972, when I began to realize the scale of the operation. Both the CIA and British Intelligence had put me under surveillance after I'd visited the American Embassy. The Soviets, realizing this, had left me alone for nearly a year, thinking that would be time enough for all interest to have cooled off. It hadn't, and through me and its own plants in the Czech Embassy DI6 knew something big was in the wind.

As the net was built up, many CIA and DI6 agents were slipped in, acting as pimps, drug pushers or porn-shop owners. Many of the homosexual cameramen were working

or the other side. Whenever a film was taken it was replaced
with other negatives, while a damaging album of STB
members was built up to be held by British Intelligence.

After Richard Bailey's death, which genuinely shocked me,
I couldn't go to the CIA or DI6 because I knew by then I
was being watched by the STB. And so I had to play along
right until the end.

How did I get my information to the CIA? Viktor's training
had been good. I used the 'brush' method often, bumping
into a CIA or DI6 agent on a busy street or Tube and passing
the message over that way. Or I would sometimes use the
back of the mirror in the ladies' toilet in the Hilton, Claridges
or the Inn on the Park. Getting the information across was no
problem. Making sure I wasn't caught was.

In return for my acting as a double agent, DI6 had promised I could keep all the earnings I made from the operation.
They broke that promise, for which I'll never forgive them.
They froze all my assets, put me through absolute hell with
God knows how many interrogations. I had to move abroad,
where thank Heavens I'd stashed some money from my private
deals with clients.

But their double-facedness made me furious and left me
with no confidence in any of the intelligence services. That's
why I'm telling you this story. To show what they're *all*
like – the Russians, Americans and British. They're all into
dirty tricks, the dirtier the better. After the way they double-
crossed me, when I had foiled the biggest subversion
operation ever attempted in Britain, can you blame me for
being angry and resentful?

Because, when you're left with almost nothing, it's hard
to forgive everything.

AFTERWORD

As stated at the beginning of this book, many details hav
been omitted for security reasons. In essence, however, th
story is complete. But there are several additional factor
which make the case important not only in terms of gainin
an insight into how foreign intelligence services operat
but also how through certain adapted attitudes, both on th
part of the public and the Government, Britain is particularl
vulnerable to operations like the one described by Sandr
Brown.

The first factor is that British Intelligence would normall
never allow an operation like Red Circle to approach any
where near its climax. Any intelligence agency in the worl
from the CIA in America to the Mossad in Israel, actin
within its own country, has the task of *preventing* the com
pletion of such events.

It is an intelligence agency's prime brief to discover wha
lies behind threats of blackmail, attempts at coercion, an
so on. The events are of no intrinsic importance. A stude
sit-in at the London School of Economics has no real im
portance in political terms. But if DI6 discover that th
'students' have been using KGB or other methods to dissemin
ate false information among genuine students, or a group
them has been receiving funds indirectly from Soviet source
then the situation becomes more relevant in terms of 'war
the spooks', or the rivalry between intelligence services. In th
United States of America, the CIA found itself the obje
of intensive investigation and criticism because the FBI ha
asked it to find out what was behind student and race rio
in the late 1960s and early 1970s.

And the reason the CIA was involved in Operation R
Circle, with the *discreet* support of DI6 and the Speci

Branch, was that both these branches of British Intelligence knew what would happen if they did become involved in any case which even hinted at invasion of privacy. They would be accused of Watergate-type tactics, and their strength seriously weakened. British Intelligence is basically afraid of a Labour Government and Socialist politicians who are only too quick to accuse it of underhand methods.

Therefore, DI6 allowed the CIA to practically take over the case between 1971 and 1973. And it was the CIA who allowed it to continue to its near climax. At present, the CIA, following a series of disclosures in various semi-underground journals, have withdrawn from such an active role in Britain, having been accused of the very things British Intelligence tried, and still tries, to avoid. The current charges against the CIA are only the beginning of an avalanche of accusations. Meanwhile, DI6 and the Special Branch must take a back seat. Thus creating an almost perfect climate for another operation along the lines of Red Circle.

STATEMENT BY SANDRA BROWN

Several years have passed since I first told Alan Radnor the story of my involvement with Operation Red Circle. I know there have been security problems and the case was studied intensively by the CIA and DI5. My only regret is that it is not possible to expose those who, unlike 'Jimmy Kingwood', were caught in the net through their own weaknesses.

For I still firmly believe that as long as you have the type of Government where politicians promise one thing and do another; where men who claim to represent the people are only building their own careers; where leaders of the country hide behind façades of respectability; when power not only corrupts them, but leaves them open to further corruption, then you will always have a 'Sandra Brown' and the beginnings of another operation in which she will be used by foreign intelligence services.

Make no mistake about this. Even as you read this now, somewhere in the world men are planning the eventual overthrow of governments. By any means.

I thought I had the answer once to the problem of showing up what I saw as the basic hypocrisy of the British system. Now, I don't know what the answer is. I'm older, not so naïve. When I look around the world, I can't see one alternative society along the lines I believed possible when I first left Glasgow.

But I'm out of it all now. I've told my story and I'm going to lead my own life. There is one other point I must make. I approached Alan Radnor while he was working on a well-known men's magazine. I did this because I knew papers like *The Sunday Times* would leave out the vital sexual elements of my story, or else water them down so much as to make them appear insignificant. Which, of course, they are not.

It's also nearly five years since Operation Red Circle took place. All the Czechs were recalled and I have no idea what happened to them. But at least I feel safe, and my 'friends' in DI5 and the CIA tell me I have no further cause to worry.

I've also turned my back on the whole world of prostitution. I'm about to be married. My future husband knows nothing of my true past. Even if he reads this book he will have no idea. As one of the CIA interrogators said, I can be very convincing!

I'm looking forward to running a home, having children, doing all the *normal* things I think I've wanted for years. My husband-to-be is an American, a member of the military. The Establishment, as I used to call it.

Crazy? Of course. But then, isn't that the story of my life?

A selection of bestsellers from SPHERE